Complementary and Alternative Medicine: Professions or Modalities?

Policy Implications for Coverage, Licensure, Scope of Practice, Institutional Privileges, and Research

Patricia M. Herman, Ian D. Coulter

Sponsored by the NCMIC Foundation

RAND
CORPORATION

For more information on this publication, visit www.rand.org/t/rr1258

Library of Congress Cataloging-in-Publication Data
is available for this publication.

ISBN: 978-0-8330-9185-7

Published by the RAND Corporation, Santa Monica, Calif.
© Copyright 2015 RAND Corporation
RAND® is a registered trademark.

Support RAND
Make a tax-deductible charitable contribution at
www.rand.org/giving/contribute

www.rand.org

Preface

The purpose of this project is to produce a RAND report/white paper on a problem that confronts the complementary and alternative medicine (CAM) professions whereby a profession is defined politically not by its full professional scope but by its treatment modalities. Even when CAM disciplines are defined by legal statutes as broad-based professions, this designation is not honored by such codes as the policies of insurance coverage. This project consisted of three parts: development of a background paper on the policy issues associated with the scope of practice and utilization of CAM practitioners in the health care system, input from a panel of CAM experts, and input from a panel of health care policy decisionmakers. The RAND report arising from this project will be available in the public domain and, therefore, be accessible to all persons with an interest in this issue. With the increasing utilization of CAM by the public and the increasing consideration of CAM in all aspects of health policy, this report will serve as a valuable reference document to aid in policymaking in terms of the challenges associated with coverage, licensure, scope of practice, institutional privileges, and research.

Contents

Acknowledgments

Funding for this project was generously provided by the NCMIC Foundation. The authors would like to acknowledge Reed Phillips and Claire Johnson for recognizing the need for this project; and Carlos Ignacio Gutierrez, a Pardee-RAND graduate student and doctoral fellow who gathered much of the information contained in this report on state statutes, guidelines and insurance coverage. We'd also like to thank Jennifer Rioux, an Ayurvedic practitioner at the University of New Mexico who specializes in whole systems methods and trial design for her input on "whole systems" studies in CAM. Finally, we would also like to acknowledge the significant contribution of our two professional panels, the members of which are listed in Appendixes A and B.

Abbreviations

ACA	Patient Protection and Affordable Care Act
ACCAHC	Academic Consortium for Complementary and Alternative Health Care
ADSM	active-duty service member
AOM	acupuncture and Oriental medicine
CAM	complementary and alternative medicine
CBO	Congressional Budget Office
CPOM	Corporate Practice of Medicine
CPT	current procedural terminology
DoD	U.S. Department of Defense
DoL	U.S. Department of Labor
E&M	evaluation and management
ICD-9	International Classification of Diseases, 9th Revision
MEPRS	Medical Expense and Performance Reporting System
MTF	military treatment facility
OPM	Office of Personnel Management
RVU	relative value unit
SSA	Social Security Act
TMD	temporomandibular disorder
VA	U.S. Department of Veterans Affairs
VHA	Veterans Health Administration

1. Introduction

One of the hallmarks of complementary and alternative medicine (CAM) is treatment of the whole person. The practitioner often evidences this this approach by addressing more than the symptom(s) (and body system[s]) of a patient's chief complaint. This broader treatment approach can involve the inclusion of patient education (e.g., on stress reduction, lifestyle improvements); monitoring of general health indicators; support, such as through a trusting patient-practitioner relationship; and the application of therapies beyond that practitioner's profession's "signature" modality—e.g., beyond spinal manipulation for chiropractors, beyond acupuncture for practitioners of Oriental medicine, beyond herbs for naturopaths. In addition, the training in some of the CAM professions includes diagnosis, appropriate referral, and other traits of primary care. These involve the provision of services (e.g., lab diagnostics, imaging, physical exams, patient counseling) also beyond the signature modality. So, for example, while traditional Chinese medicine, naturopathic medicine, and chiropractic medicine all have a modality that is a core part of their scope (i.e., acupuncture, natural herbs, and manipulation, respectively) and by which they are strongly identified, that modality is delivered within a broad paradigm that will include a range of wellness interventions such as stress management, exercise, nutrition, weight management, posture, and preventive care.

Although CAM has this whole person approach, and even when the CAM profession has broad primary care training, CAM is generally addressed in terms of procedures (modalities or therapies) in research and policy. Although this problem is described as one of terminology, even a problem of semantics, it is not just a problem of definition/perception. Policies that define a profession only in terms of its therapeutic modalities, or reduce a profession's scope to only some of these modalities, have direct impacts on patient access and care. Last, but not least, these policies have significant political consequences as these groups strive to obtain full legal and social legitimization. Where the profession does have full legislative recognition as a profession but is prevented from exercising the privileges associated with that recognition, a case could be made that the legislative intent is being thwarted—e.g., Medicare covering chiropractors only for certain licensed services and not for others, even though these other services are covered when offered by other providers.

Broadly speaking, there are at least two perspectives that dominate this issue. On the one hand is the perspective of the CAM professions, both those fully recognized and those still struggling to obtain legislative recognition. On the other hand is the perspective of those who must formulate policy around the inclusion of CAM in health services. In this report we will examine the way in which both groups view the issues.

Organization of this Report

As background, we will start by presenting the topic of this paper in terms used in sociology—i.e., whether CAM practitioners are treated in policy as members of a profession or as providers of a particular skill (procedure). We will then present the types of CAM addressed in this report, and give examples of the types of policy where the issue of profession or procedure/modality comes up. This will be followed by a summary of the results of the CAM expert panel meeting and a summary of the health policy decisionmakers panel meeting. We will end with a summary of the main issues identified.

2. Background on Professions versus Procedures

Sociology provides one perspective on the difference between a profession and a skill occupation (the provider of a procedure or modality). A profession can be defined sociologically as *a social group that has exclusive access to knowledge and skills, is autonomous, self-regulating, has authority, controls entry, is regulated by the state, and has exclusive powers and/or rights.*[1] A nonprofessional (skill) occupation may have some of these characteristics, but not all, and not to the degree of the profession. Note that sociology also recognizes that the definition of a profession is a moving target, a process, and that professional status exists on a continuum with different groups achieving different levels of each of these characteristics at different points in their history.[2] Finally, sociology sees the achievement of professional status as a very political process that often involves a struggle for power.

Professionalization as a Political Process

Historically, professions arose out of guilds and were given extraordinary independence, authority and power by the state. This occurred through what has come to be called the social contract. In return for certain responsibilities, the professions were given extensive powers and privileges. In the health field this could be the power to control entry to the profession, to accredit the institutions of education and training, to discipline members, to disbar members, to set standards, to claim exclusivity for practices/modalities, to conduct human dissection, to prosecute any others who might trespass on their scope of practice, and to virtually define what constitutes health, acceptable health care, and healing.[3] The most extensive power in the health system was given to allopathic medicine, and with it, medical doctors have historically been able to confront and prosecute any whom they deemed were practicing medicine without a license, including most CAM practitioners. While this level of authority has been steadily reduced for allopathic medicine, the medical profession still retains considerable power.

Few other social institutions outside of professions were given this level of power and authority. Therefore, the question sociology would pose is: Why did the state do this?[4] Some might argue that it was done in recognition of the beneficence the professions provided for the public. While that is partly true, it would be naïve to suggest this was the only reason. As part of

---

[1] R. D. Mootz, I. D. Coulter, and G. D. Schultz, "Professionalism and Ethics in Chiropractic," in *Principles and Practices of Chiropractic*, S. Haldeman, ed., New York: McGraw Hill, 2005, pp. 201–219.

[2] E. Greenwood, "Attributes of a Profession," *Social Work*, Vol. 2, No. 3, 1957, pp. 45–55.

[3] Mootz, Coulter, and Schultz, 2005.

[4] D. Salhani and I. D. Coulter, "The Politics of Interprofessional Working and the Struggle for Professional Autonomy in Nursing," *Social Science and Medicine*, Vol. 68, No. 7, 2009, pp. 1221–1228.

the social contract all health professions, for example, accept that their primary responsibility is to their patients and agree to act in the interest of the patients and the public even at the expense of their own interest. This agreement required that each profession adopt a code of ethics and take an oath (such as the Hippocratic oath taken by all doctors). But it is also the case that a profession (through being a formal group with internally consistent goals) could lobby and organize to win special privileges. So the professions actually accrued power through a highly political process involving negotiations between the state and the professions. At certain times in history the balance of power lay with the professions. Currently, the power of professions is waning, and the state has taken back much of the power and authority professions once had.

It should also be noted that as opposed to the classic professions (medicine, law, clergy, etc.) that all addressed different social needs, the CAM disciplines are trying to be established as professions, with all the attendant powers and privileges, within the same social topic area (health) as conventional medicine. Therefore, even though most of CAM flourishes by providing services not provided (or, some claim, not adequately provided) by conventional medicine, every power and privilege given by the state to a CAM profession can be interpreted as taking away some of the powers and privileges (i.e., cutting into the monopoly) of conventional medicine.[5] So, in the pursuit of professional autonomy, negotiations are not just between the CAM profession and the state; they are also between the various professions addressing the human need called health. Historically, this has not been an amicable dialogue.

In summary, professionalism is a social construct shaped through a political process, and what the state has the power to give, it also can also take away. Professions that have won privileges may lose them again. Professions still without desired privileges must constantly lobby, organize, and persuade those who grant the privileges to act on their behalf. Patients can, of course, be recruited to help in this process.

One of our major concerns is that even groups that have achieved political legitimacy, that have attained all the characteristics associated with professions and are generally thought of as professions, are still reduced to modalities within many aspects of health care policy. Therefore, our focus reflects the caution that achieving professional status is not per se a guarantee that policies will work to their advantage. This is important for those already in this position but is crucially important for those groups still seeking full recognition as professions.

---

[5] Greenwood, 1957.

3. CAM Professions Represented in This Report

In this document we limit our discussion to the types of CAM whose practitioners have licensure in at least one state, which includes those with the strongest claim on professional status. This does not mean that this report will not be of use to other CAM disciplines. All CAM professions will encounter the types of policies discussed in this report that might affect their practice and will have to consider the steps required to structure their practice environment in ways their profession thinks is most appropriate.

The number and range of CAM professions are large, and addressing them all is beyond the scope of this report. Therefore, we have chosen to generally use the criteria used to define the core membership of the Academic Consortium for Complementary and Alternative Health Care (ACCAHC) to determine the types of CAM addressed in this report. According to the ACCAHC website, core member CAM disciplines "have an accrediting agency recognized by the U.S. Department of Education, have a recognized certification or testing organization, and are licensed for professional practice in at least one state." The CAM disciplines included in ACCAHC core membership and this report are

- acupuncture and Oriental medicine
- chiropractic
- massage therapy
- naturopathic medicine.

Note that direct-entry midwifery is part of ACCAHC's core membership and meets many of the criteria for being a profession. While they are primary maternity care providers of birth in homes and free-standing birth centers, as an alternative to in-hospital birth, they are not typically considered either at the National Institutes of Health or in general discussions as part of the CAM inclusion dialogue. Therefore, we will not focus on this profession in this document.

The ACCAHC core member criteria directly address two of the criteria for a profession (control of entry into the field through a recognized certification or testing organization, and state recognition through licensure). ACCAHC's criteria also cover other professional aspects of self-regulation and of education and training quality by requiring a Department of Education-recognized accrediting agency. Table 3.1 presents some of the characteristics of these four CAM disciplines. The last row of this table indicates whether each participated in writing a document titled "Meeting the Nation's Primary Care Needs." This document was developed and written

acupuncture, virtually all states use licensure; for massage, there is a mixture of licensing, certification, and registration statutes." Also, the number of licensed states for naturopathic medicine has been corrected from that listed in the Desk Reference with the recent passage of licensure legislation in Maryland.

SOURCES: Goldblatt et al., 2013;Goldstein and Weeks, 2013; and various state websites.

As can be seen from this table, each of the five CAM disciplines shown meets at least some of the criteria for a profession—that is, they are in various places along the continuum toward the classic definition of a profession. Based on the information on the level of education required, professional authority, and primary care focus, and given its recognition in all states, the strongest case for a profession can be made for chiropractic, with naturopathic medicine and acupuncture and Oriental Medicine close behind—each with recognition in fewer states. Massage therapy probably has the furthest to go to claim being a profession. For example, massage therapy did not participate in the ACCAHC document discussing the role of CAM disciplines in providing primary care, and a massage therapy license does not require extensive education and training. A recent document laying out the future massage therapy research agenda also noted challenges such as the inconsistency of quality in entry-level massage therapy education, that schools have multiple options for accreditation, and differences between the two national licensing examinations.[1] Nevertheless, we will address and include discussion relating to massage therapy in this report where appropriate and relevant.

---

[1] J. R. Kahn and M. B. Menard, *Massage Therapy Research Agenda: 2015 and Beyond*, Evanston, Ill.: Massage Therapy Foundation, 2014.

4. Examples of Policies Where Profession versus Procedures Makes a Difference

There are a number of different types of health-related policies where designation as a profession versus as a procedure or modality has an impact. We identified licensure, research funding, treatment guidelines, health plan coverage, and workforce issues as key policy areas. The information contained in this chapter, as well as the previous ones, was provided to the CAM expert panelists in advance of their panel meeting as a briefing paper and a starting place for discussions. The panelists were asked to comment on the briefing paper, and their comments were incorporated here where appropriate. The panelists provided more detail in a number of the policy areas, but especially contributed to the text on workforce issues.

Licensure

The four CAM disciplines discussed in this paper are all licensed at least in some states—see Table 3.1. These laws are one means by which the states can be seen as bestowing authority, rights, and privileges on a profession. We examined the language used in a sample of two states' laws to get an idea of how each discipline is discussed, focusing on scope of practice and whether any of this scope is exclusive. Although the language used in each state is unique, we started by looking at the laws in California and Texas as exemplars and searched for the licensure statutes pertaining to acupuncture, chiropractic, naturopathic, and massage in each state's code. We then, as mentioned earlier in the section on the CAM expert panel, supplemented this information with comments provided by those panelists.

Note that individual states set the scope of practice for the health care professions practicing in that state. Comments from the CAM expert panel noted that for a profession to have a national presence there needs to be consistency across states in the authority, rights and privileges bestowed by licensure.[2] There also has to be consistency in education and training requirements across states. Although our review of licensure statutes here is brief, it is still evident that a CAM profession's scope of practice can vary widely across states.

Acupuncture and Oriental Medicine

The profession of Oriental medicine is mentioned in these laws, but most of the text addresses the procedure called acupuncture. However, it is interesting that the term acupuncture is considered to include acupuncture in combination with a number of other therapies. For example, in Texas, the term acupuncture includes "the administration of thermal or electrical treatments or the recommendation of dietary guidelines, energy flow exercise, or dietary or

---

[2] S. Stumpf, "Acupuncture Practice Acts: A Profession's Growing Pains," *Explore*, Vol. 11, No. 3, May–June 2015, pp. 217–221.

herbal supplements in conjunction with" the acupuncture itself.[3] In California, an acupuncturist's license authorizes the holder to "perform or prescribe the use of Asian massage, acupressure, breathing techniques, exercise, heat, cold, magnets, nutrition, diet, herbs, plant, animal, and mineral products, and dietary supplements to promote, maintain, and restore health" in addition to engaging in the practice of acupuncture.[4] The authors of a recent article on acupuncture research comment that the term acupuncture "has been used to refer to either a specific procedure involving acupuncture needling or a multicomponent treatment that also involves history taking, physical examination, diagnosis, and education."[5] Note that the New Mexico law has one of the most comprehensive scopes of practice for acupuncture and Oriental medicine (AOM) in the country.

AOM practitioners do not always have autonomy, one of the privileges of a profession, to determine who should see them and the appropriate length of treatment. For example, in Texas, an acupuncturist can "perform acupuncture on a person for smoking addiction, weight loss, alcoholism, chronic pain, or substance abuse."[6] However, all other conditions require a referral from a physician, a dentist, or a chiropractor. Also, for any condition other than smoking addiction and weight loss, the acupuncturist must "refer the person to a physician after performing acupuncture 20 times or for two months" if no substantial improvement occurs in the condition for which the referral was made.[7]

Chiropractic Medicine

Chiropractors in California seem to be licensed more as a profession than those in Texas. In both California and Texas chiropractors are allowed to manipulate and adjust the musculoskeletal system, and they have the authority to diagnosis and treat. However, in Texas this authority is restricted to the musculoskeletal system.[8] In contrast, in California, chiropractors may diagnose and "treat any condition, disease, or injury [. . .] so long as such treatment or diagnosis is done in a manner consistent with chiropractic methods and techniques and so long as such methods and treatment do not constitute the practice of medicine by exceeding the legal scope of chiropractic practice as set forth in this section."[9] Examples of what would exceed

---

[3] State of Texas, *Texas Occupations Code—Chapter 205 Acupuncture,* 2011a, p. 1.

[4] State of California, *Business and Professions Code Section 4935–4949,* "Acupuncture Certification Requirements," Section 4937, 2014a.

[5] H. M. Langevin, P. M Wayne, H. MacPherson, R. Schnyer, R. M. Milley, V. Napadow, L. Lao, J. Park, R. E. Harris, and M. Cohen, "Paradoxes in Acupuncture Research: Strategies for Moving Forward" *Evidence-Based Complementary and Alternative Medicine, 2011,* 2011, pp. 1–11. Quoted material from p. 3.

[6] State of Texas, *Board Rules,* Texas Administrative Code, Title 22, Part 9, Chapter 183, Rule §183.7, 2014.

[7] State of Texas, 2014.

[8] State of Texas, *Occupations Code—Chapter 201 Chiropractors,* Subchapter A. General Provisions, Section 201.002, 2011b.

[9] State of California, *Rules and Regulations,* "Board of Chiropractic Examiners, Editor," 2013a, p. 4.

chiropractic's legal scope in California include surgery, childbirth, dentistry, optometry, prescription medicine, and mammography. In California chiropractors are allowed to "use all necessary mechanical, hygienic, and sanitary measures incident to the care of the body, including, but not limited to, air, cold, diet, exercise, heat, light, massage, physical culture, rest, ultrasound, water, and physical therapy techniques in the course of chiropractic manipulations and/or adjustments."[10]

Naturopathic Medicine

Naturopathic medicine is licensed in California (and 16 other states), but not in Texas. In Texas, anyone can call him- or herself a naturopathic doctor.[11] "Naturopathy" is also illegal in two states: South Carolina[12] and Tennessee.[13] The broadest scope of practice for naturopaths is found in Oregon, Washington, Arizona, Vermont, and Hawaii. Where naturopathic medicine practitioners are licensed, they tend to have a broad scope of practice that includes the authority to diagnose and treat, use a variety of modalities, and, in some states, prescribe drugs. In general, the focus is on the privileges and authority of this profession, with much less discussion of specific procedures. For example, in California, naturopathic medicine is defined as "a distinct and comprehensive system of primary health care practiced by a naturopathic doctor for the diagnosis, treatment, and prevention of human health conditions, injuries, and disease."[14]

Massage Therapy

In California massage therapists must be certified, and in Texas massage therapists are licensed. Although sometimes certification is considered voluntary and licensure mandatory, all massage therapists (and massage practitioners) in California must be certified as such to practice.[15] Massage therapy seems to be exclusively treated as a procedure in its certification and licensure laws. The laws in both states clearly state that massage therapists cannot diagnose and treat, and they keep the definition of what constitutes massage fairly narrow, spending many more words on what massage therapists cannot do.[16]

---

[10] State of California, 2013a, p. 4.

[11] Texas Association of Naturopathic Doctors, *FAQ*, 2014.

[12] South Carolina Code of Laws, Title 40, Chapter 31.

[13] 2010 Tennessee Code, Title 63, Chapter 6, Part 2, 63-6-205, amended 2012.

[14] State of California, *Business and Professions Code, Division 2, Chapter 8.2, Article 1*, "Naturopathic Doctors Act," Section 3613, 2013b.

[15] State of California, *Business and Professions Code, Division 2, Chapter 10.5*, "Massage Therapy Act," Section 4611, 2014b.

[16] State of California, 2014b, Section 4609; State of Texas, *Occupations Code—Chapter 455 Massage Therapy*, Subchapter A. General Provisions, Section 455.001-3, 1999.

Research

One reason to do research is to inform policy. Although most researchers would like research to have a larger impact on policy, many would probably agree that research is necessary, although not sufficient, for policy change. Given the potential influence of research on policy, in this section we will briefly review how each CAM discipline is characterized in its research. In general, if policies are to be made regarding these disciplines as professions—i.e., granting rights and recognizing the authority of the body of knowledge embodied in these practitioners versus policies addressing the use of the procedures or therapies these practitioners can provide— research that addresses the effectiveness and safety of the profession, rather than just of its procedures, is needed. For example, research should answer "what is the impact of going to a chiropractor?" rather than "what is the impact of spinal manipulation?" Note that funding policies affect the types of research funded, so policy affects research, and research affects policy.

The study of the impact of a discipline or profession is often called whole systems or whole practice research and is considered part of health services research.[17] Much of health services research utilizes effectiveness studies, which look at whether something works in the real world. These types of studies stand in stark contrast to those intended to determine efficacy (whether something can work under strictly controlled conditions).[18] Efficacy studies are usually confined to studies of specific well-defined therapies (procedures) and, almost by definition, are not appropriate to measure the impact of a profession. Effectiveness studies are more appropriate for the study of a profession. However, most of these also only look at the addition of a procedure or therapy. Overall, the vast majority of research dollars in CAM go to studies of individual therapies or procedures. Although there is growing interest in whole systems or whole practice research, it is still true that very little funding goes to studies of the impact of CAM professions. Because studies that measure the effect of a patient going to a practitioner of a particular profession are rare, below we provide an illustrative example of a study that could be considered to measure the impact of each CAM profession.

---

[17] P. M. Herman, K. D'Huyvetter, and M. J. Mohler, "Are Health Services Research Methods a Match for CAM?" *Alternative Therapies in Health and Medicine*, Vol. 12, No. 3, 2006, p. 78–83; C. Ritenbaugh, M. Verhoef, S. Fleishman, H. Boon, and A. Leis, "Whole Systems Research: A Discipline for Studying Complementary and Alternative Medicine," *Alternative Therapies in Health and Medicine*, Vol. 9, No. 4, 2002, pp. 32–36.

[18] G. Gartlehner, R. A. Hansen, D. Nissman, D. N, Lohr, and T. S. Carey, "Criteria for Distinguishing Effectiveness from Efficacy Trials in Systematic Reviews," in *Technical Reviews*, Rockville, Md.: Agency for Healthcare Research and Quality, 2006.

Acupuncture and Oriental Medicine

AOM has invested extensive time and effort in efficacy research for acupuncture, including creating two documents to guide researchers on how to report on acupuncture studies.[19] However, a recent article reviewing AOM research recommends that the profession also incorporate whole systems studies.[20] Following is an example of a whole systems (profession-level) study of AOM and naturopathic medicine.

> A whole-systems approach was used in designing the CAM interventions. TCM [traditional Chinese medicine] and NM [naturopathic medicine] clinicians and investigators collaboratively developed treatment protocols for each CAM intervention arm. These protocols were developed from literature reviews as well as community best practices, based on input from study practitioners and outside experts, with the intention of maintaining the theoretical perspective of each system of care. Next, the protocols were converted to study practitioner written guidelines that specified treatment parameters. Most importantly, in both arms, practitioners were to treat all aspects of the patient, not just the TMD, in a manner consistent with their medical systems. The two complementary and alternative medicine interventions were designed to be matched to each other in total contact time (9–10 hours total) and intervention time frame (3–4 months). In practice, however, the time frame for the TCM arm extended to 5–6 months and for the NM arm to 8 months.[21]

Chiropractic Medicine

Since chiropractic has been covered by various health plans longer than the other CAM professions, a substantial portion of chiropractic research has examined the impact of going to a chiropractic doctor versus a conventional practitioner for care for musculoskeletal conditions. These studies can all be considered studies of the effectiveness of the chiropractic profession, even though generally limited to individuals with musculoskeletal conditions. However, there have also been a number of efficacy studies of spinal manipulation itself. In contrast, here is an example of a whole practice (profession-level) study of chiropractic:

> The study physicians provided a variety of health services. The salient features of chiropractic care were spinal manipulation, physical therapy, exercise plan, and

---

[19] H. MacPherson, D. G. Altman, R. Hammerschlag, L. Youping, W. Taixiang, A. White, and D. Moher, "Revised Standards for Reporting Interventions in Clinical Trials of Acupuncture (STRICTA): Extending the CONSORT Statement," *Journal of Evidence-Based Medicine*, Vol. 3, No. 3, 2010, pp. 140–155; H. MacPherson, A. White, M. Cummings, K. A. Jobst, K. Rose, and R. C. Niemtzow, "Standards for Reporting Interventions in Controlled Trials of Acupuncture: The STRICTA Recommendations" *Journal of Alternative and Complementary Medicine*, Vol. 8, No. 1, 2002 pp. 85–89.

[20] Langevin et al., 2011.

[21] C. Ritenbaugh, R. Hammerschlag, C. Calabrese, S. Mist, M. Aickin, E. Sutherland, J. Leben, L. DeBar, C. Elder, and S. F. Dworkin, "A Pilot Whole Systems Clinical Trial of Traditional Chinese Medicine and Naturopathic Medicine for the Treatment of Temporomandibular Disorders," *Journal of Alternative and Complementary Medicine*, Vol. 14, No. 5, 2008, pp. 475–487. Quoted material from p. 477.

self-care education. Medical patients received prescription drugs, exercise plan, and self-care advice. About 25% were referred for physical therapy.[22]

Naturopathic Medicine

Naturopathic medicine is not so clearly identified by a signature modality as the other CAM professions are. Each of the different modalities used has its own set of efficacy and effectiveness studies. Most of the studies of naturopathic medicine itself are whole systems or whole practice (profession-level) studies. The temporomandibular disorder (TMD) study above (under AOM) and the study following are examples of effectiveness studies of the profession of naturopathic medicine:

> For consistency with naturopathic practice, treatment recommendations were individualized from a predetermined menu of interventions based on which risk factors were present and patient preferences. Therapies included specific diet and lifestyle recommendations and the prescription of selected natural health products.[23]

Massage Therapy

Although massage is often seen as one type of treatment or procedure, there are many types of massage, and each of these types may be (and many have been) subject to its own tests of efficacy. Next is an example of what could be considered a study of the massage profession:

> Individuals in the massage group (Clinic B) met with a registered massage therapist (RMT) on the first week of the program to set up a weekly massage schedule. This protocol is based on typical treatment plans used by massage therapists for novice runners. The first 1 h session (week 1) included overall evaluation by the RMT, recommendations for future individualized massage sessions, education and massage. Subsequent weekly 30 min massage sessions (9 weeks) focused on individual massage needs for each subject as assessed and recorded by their RMT. Each subject was assigned to one of four participating RMTs for the duration of the study. All RMTs were registered massage therapists with the College of Massage Therapists of Ontario and had received the necessary training and passed the qualification examinations necessary for such accreditation. All possessed a range from 3 to 13 years' experience in the realm of sport massage and had received further sports massage training in an accredited sport medicine clinic.
>
> It was important that each subject received an individualized treatment program (that was recorded) rather than a standardized protocol since this focused on

---

[22] M. Haas B. Goldberg, M. Aickin, B. Ganger, and M. Attwood, "A Practice-Based Study of Patients with Acute and Chronic Low Back Pain Attending Primary Care and Chiropractic Physicians: Two-Week to 48-Month Follow-Up," *Journal of Manipulative and Physiological Therapeutics*, Vol. 27, No. 3, 2004, pp. 160–169. Quoted material from p. 163.

[23] D. Seely, O. Szczurko, K. Cooley, H. Fritz, S. Aberdour, C. Herrington, P. Herman, P. Rouchotas, D. Lescheid, and R. Bradley, "Naturopathic Medicine for the Prevention of Cardiovascular Disease: A Randomized Clinical Trial, *Canadian Medical Association Journal*, Vol. 185, No. 9, 2013, pp. E409–E416. Quoted material from p. E410.

individual needs of the participant and is the form of treatment that actually takes place in regular massage practice. Although the treatments were individualized to each participant in order to maximize the external validity of the study, all treatments utilized common Swedish massage techniques. Based on the individual treatment plan for each participant, the therapy included a combination of stretching, passive, active, and resisted range of motion exercises, muscle energy techniques, trigger point and fascial release, compression work, petrissage, and effleurage massage strokes. [24]

Treatment Guidelines

Treatment guidelines are written by various groups within the health care system and indicate, for a particular condition, the therapies recommended for treatment. These recommendations are generally based on the therapies for which the research shows the most evidence of efficacy or effectiveness.

We mainly reviewed U.S. guidelines for conditions for which CAM is most used, according to the 2007 National Health Interview Survey.[25] In all cases the US-based guidelines refer to procedures, not to professions. For example, several guidelines include recommendations for spinal manipulation,[26] acupuncture[27], and massage.[28] In contrast, we found one Canadian

---

[24] K. A. Dawson, L. Dawson, A. Thomas, and P. M. Tiidus, "Effectiveness of Regular Proactive Massage Therapy for Novice Recreational Runners, *Physical Therapy in Sport*, Vol. 12, No. 4, 2011, p. 182–187. Quoted material from pp. 184–185.

[25] P. M. Barnes, B. Bloom, and R. L. Nahin, "Complementary and Alternative Medicine Use Among Adults and Children: United States, 2007," in *National Health Statistics Reports*, Hyattsville, Md., 2008.

[26] B. W. Koes, M. van Tulder, C.-W. C. Lin, L. G. Macedo, J. McAuley, and C. Maher, "An Updated Overview of Clinical Guidelines for the Management of Non-Specific Low Back Pain in Primary Care," *European Spine Journal*, Vol. 19, No. 12, 2010. pp. 2075–2094; A. Delitto, S. Z. George, L. Van Dillen, J. M. Whitman, G. Sowa, P. Shekelle, T. R. Denninger, and J. J. Godges, "Low Back Pain Clinical Practice Guidelines Linked to the International Classification of Functioning, Disability, and Health," *Journal of Orthopedic Sports Physical Therapy*, Vol. 42, No. 4, 2012, pp. A1–A57; R. Chou, A. Qaseem, V. Snow, D. Casey, J. T. Cross, P. Shekelle, and D. K. Owens, "Diagnosis and Treatment of Low Back Pain: A Joint Clinical Practice Guideline from the American College of Physicians and the American Pain Society," *Annals of Internal Medicine*, Vol. 147, No. 7, 2007, pp. 478–491; R. Chou, "In the Clinic: Low Back Pain," *Annals of Internal Medicine*, 2014, pp. 1–16; J. Guzman, D. S. Haldeman, L. J. Carroll, E. J. Carragee, E. L. Hurwitz, M. P. Peloso, M. Nordin, J. D. Cassidy, L. W. Holm, P. Cote, J. van der Velde, and S. Hogg-Johnson, "Clinical Practice Implications of the Bone and Joint Decade 2000–2010 Task Force on Neck Pain and Its Associated Disorders: From Concepts and Findings to Recommendations," *Spine*, Vol. 33, No. 45, 2008, pp. S199–S213; J. D. Childs, J. A. Cleland, J. M. Elliott, D. S. Teyhen, R. S. Wainner, J. M. Whitman, B. J. Sopky, J. J. Godges, T. W. Flynn, and A. Delitto, "Neck Pain: Clinical Practice Guidelines Linked to the International Classification of Functioning, Disability, and Health from the Orthopaedic Section of the American Physical Therapy Association," *Journal of Orthopedic Sports Physical Therapy*, Vol. 38, No. 9, 2008, pp. A1–A34; S. D. Silberstein, "Practice Parameter: Evidence-Based Guidelines for Migraine Headache (an Evidence-Based Review): Report of the Quality Standards Subcommittee of the American Academy of Neurology," *Neurology*, Vol. 55, No. 6, 2000, pp. 754–762; University of Texas. *Management of Fibromyalgia Syndrome in Adults*, Family Nurse Practitioner Program, 2009.

[27] Chou et al., 2007; Chou, 2014; Guzman et al., 2008; Silberstein 2000; University of Texas, 2009; American Society of Anesthesiologists Task Force on Chronic Pain Management, "Practice Guidelines for Chronic Pain Management," *Anesthesiology*, Vol. 112, No. 4, 2010, pp. 1–24; American Psychiatric Association, *Practice*

guideline for back pain[29] that recommended referral to "a trained spinal care specialist." The document went on to list the professions included in that designation, and this list included chiropractors.

Health Plan Coverage

Health plan coverage is one of the policy areas of most interest to CAM providers. The determination of who and what is covered seems to be made based on three things: profession/license of the practitioner (and whether that individual is part of the health plan's network), the procedure being offered (and the Current Procedural Terminology [CPT] codes the practitioner is allowed to bill), and the condition (the International Classification of Diseases 9th Revision [ICD-9] diagnosis code) for which the treatment is given. Different health plans cover different combinations of these three characteristics for a health care encounter. Sometimes instead of covering particular procedures, a health plan will allow coverage of care by a provider type (profession) up to a particular dollar amount per year. A detailed analysis of coverage is beyond the scope of this report. However, we will make a few salient points about these three dimensions.

Profession/License of the Practitioner

Often health plans will cover the services of only some types of providers (i.e., providers within some professions, and these providers are often required to contract with the health plan).

In 1995 Washington state passed a law called the Every Category of Health Care Providers Law, or WAC 284-43-205, which states that "health carriers (health insurance plans/payers) shall not exclude any category of providers licensed by the state of Washington who provide health care services or care within the scope of their practice. . . . " The law requires the plans to provide patient/member access to every **category** *of provider* (as distinct from *every provider*) licensed to treat any condition enumerated in Washington's basic health benefit package. This has resulted in coverage in the state for the services of chiropractors, naturopathic doctors, acupuncturists, and massage therapists.

Affordable Care Act

On March 23, 2010, President Obama signed the Patient Protection and Affordable Care Act (ACA) into law. Section 2706 of this law is titled *Non-Discrimination in Health Care*, and Part A of this section says,

---

Guideline for the Treatment of Patients with Major Depressive Disorder, 3rd ed., Arlington, Va.: American Psychiatric Association, 2010.

[28] Chou et al., 2007; Chou, 2014; University of Texas, 2009.

[29] Toward Optimized Practice. *Guideline for the Evidence-Informed Primary Care Management of Low Back Pain*, 2011.

22

> A group health plan and a health insurance issuer offering group or individual health insurance coverage shall not discriminate with respect to participation under the plan or coverage against any health care provider who is acting within the scope of that provider's license or certification under applicable State law.[30]

At first glance this wording (inserted into the Senate bill with the help of Sen. Tom Harkin) looks as if it would support expanded coverage of CAM. However, the law goes on to say,

> This section shall not require that a group health plan or health insurance issuer contract with any health care provider willing to abide by the terms and conditions for participation established by the plan or issuer.[31]

So on the one hand Section 2706(a) opens an avenue for expanded use of licensed or certified nonphysician providers (including CAM providers) in a wide range of health plans and insurance products;[32] however, it is written in such a way that it may not change coverage decisions as much as hoped.

Procedure Codes

Providers often bill (ask for reimbursement from) a health plan using CPT codes to describe the services rendered. At present there are specific CPT codes for massage (97124; 15 minutes), acupuncture (97810, 97811, 97813, and 97814; 15 minutes each, initial and reinsertion of the needles, with and without electrical stimulation), and chiropractic (98940–43; number of spinal regions adjusted or if extraspinal) procedures. Note that in contrast to the massage and acupuncture CPT codes, which can be used by any practitioner licensed to provide those services, the chiropractic codes are specific for use by chiropractors.

There are also many other procedures practiced by CAM providers that are within the scope of practice of these providers, but for which no CPT code exists (e.g., for moxibustion or cupping used in AOM), or for which reimbursement may not be allowed.

It seems that some health plans allow CAM practitioners to bill for evaluation and management (E&M; the "99" codes), which covers services such as history taking and physical exam, patient education/guidance/counseling, the ordering of diagnostic/imaging studies, and the development of a treatment plan. Being able to bill to these E&M codes seems to be a rough indicator of whether the practitioner is being treated as a professional (a member of a profession trained in patient evaluation and management—i.e., a doctor or "patient manager"). Chiropractors have been working with the Centers for Medicare and Medicaid Services (CMS) to be allowed to charge E&M codes when appropriate for their office visits.[33] E&M codes are

---

[30] *Non-Discrimination in Health Care*, in *42 U.S.Code § 300gg-5.* 2010.

[31] 42 U. S. C. *§ 300gg-5*, 2010.

[32] J. D. Blum, "Non-Discrimination and the Role of Complementary and Alternative Medicine," *BNA's Health Law Reporter*, Vol., 23, 2014, pp. 1–5.

[33] J. Weeks, "Chiropractic Doctors Hit a Trifecta in Move for 'Cultural Authority'," *The Integrator Blog*, 2013.

generally appropriate for a new patient, when reevaluating a current patient after a treatment plan has been implemented, or when a current patient presents with a new injury or condition.

As mentioned above, sometimes health plans reimburse for services of a profession up to a certain dollar amount each year. In these cases, procedure codes are not needed. However, other types of problems arise. Since all procedures done by the provider, including labs and imaging, are included under the dollar limit for that provider, the practitioner has to choose to use some of the dollar allocation on (needed) testing and possibly not order all needed tests, or to delay care by sending the patient back to his or her primary MD provider to order the tests.

Note that health plans may like limiting CPT codes to one type of provider or provider type–specific spending caps simply because it is easier for them to perform utilization reviews and implement the caps, since they have to look at only a single data field—provider type.

Limits on the Covered Conditions

Often a health plan will put limits on the types of conditions for which a particular CAM procedure is covered. For example, the Kaiser California Gold HMO plan will cover acupuncture provided by a participating licensed acupuncturist, but only for a neuromusculoskeletal disorder, nausea, or pain.[34] This same plan limits chiropractic coverage to participating chiropractors offering chiropractic services determined to be medically necessary to treat or diagnose a neuromusculoskeletal disorder.

Another related challenge for AOM is the translation of their diagnostic system (e.g., liver qi constraint, wind-heat external pathogenic factor) into the diagnoses recognized by the conventional health care system (e.g., ICD-9 codes).

Public Plans (Medicare, Veterans Health Administration, TRICARE)

Here we briefly review what is known about coverage offered to CAM providers under the public programs. Some of the barriers to coverage are addressed in the next section on workforce issues.

Medicare

At this time the only CAM provider type covered by Medicare (Part B) is chiropractic, and only for one procedure: chiropractic manipulative treatment involving one or two, three or four, or five regions of the spine, CPT codes 98940, 98941, and 98942, respectively.

---

[34] Kaiser Permanente, *2014 Disclosure Form for Kaiser Permanente Small Business Gold 0/30 Copayment HMO Plan*, Oakland, Calif.: Kaiser Permanente, 2014, p. 64.

Veterans Health Administration

The 2011 Veterans Health Administration (VHA) report indicates that CAM therapies, including acupuncture and massage, are offered at 90 percent of VHA facilities.[35] This report also notes that chiropractic care is so well embedded into the VHA that it has been reclassified as a mainstream practice and is no longer considered CAM. Nevertheless, the only information we were able to find on coverage of CAM at the VHA is the following:

> Individual eligibility determinations are difficult, and therefore outside the scope of this general information. Please contact your local VA health care facility for individual veteran eligibility questions or concerns.[36]

TRICARE

TRICARE is the health care program that covers uniformed service members and their families.[37] In general, TRICARE does not cover CAM for active-duty service members (ADSMs) when supplied by providers outside military treatment facilities (MTFs)—i.e., from civilian providers. However, TRICARE does acknowledge that acupuncture may be offered at some MTFs and approved for certain ADSMs, and notes that coverage for chiropractic care is limited to ADSMs and is available at only specific MTFs under the Chiropractic Care Program. TRICARE also specifically excludes naturopathy and massage from coverage.

Workforce Issues

There are a number of different policy issues that affect whether and how CAM providers are included in the health care workforce. Some of these have been covered earlier (e.g., licensure, insurance coverage); however, a number of other issues also have an effect.

Provider Types Allowed in Medicare

Medicare is allowed to reimburse care for only a physician's services as defined in the Social Security Act (Section 1861), and chiropractors are included in that definition of a physician. For other provider types to be covered by Medicare, this act would have to be changed (by an act of Congress) to include those provider types. In addition to this affecting Medicare coverage, many other health-related policies are based on whether a profession type is covered under Medicare. For example, some state Medicaid systems limit coverage to the provider types covered by Medicare, the U.S. Department of Veterans Affairs (VA) reimburses for outside care based on Medicare's guidelines, some medical education loan repayment programs limit eligibility to providers covered by Medicare, and residency funding is tied to appropriations for Medicare.

---

[35] Healthcare Analysis and Information Group, *2011 Complementary and Alternative Medicine Survey*, Department of Veterans Affairs, Washington, D.C.: Veterans Health Administration, 2011.

[36] U.S. Department of Veterans Affairs, *Pre-Authorized Outpatient Medical Care*, 2011.

[37] TRICARE, *Tricare*, 2014a; TRICARE, *Tricare Provider Handbook*, 2014b.

Practice within the VA and DoD/TRICARE

The VHA and the medical health system of the Department of Defense (DoD) both hire doctors and other health care providers on a salaried basis. To do this, both organizations use the Office of Personnel Management (OPM) job code lists. At present these lists do not include specific categories for CAM providers. However, they do include categories that have been used to hire CAM practitioners. For example, the Department of the Army hired a licensed acupuncturist as a GS-0601-12 (General Health Science Series [0601], Level 12). The basic requirements of the 0601 series are that the individual have a degree that demonstrates "major study in an academic field related to the health sciences or allied sciences appropriate to the work of the position."[38] The VA also uses the OPM classification scheme and has hired a licensed acupuncturist as a GS-0640-07—Health Technician (0640), Level 07 (information from USAJobs, the Federal Government's Official Job Site). The basic requirements for a Health Technician are said to "range widely in type and include support duties to medical or health personnel such as audiologists, speech pathologists, medical officers, and optometrists."[39] However, Health Technicians hired at level 05 and above must have "successful completion of a full 4-year course of study leading to a bachelor's degree, with major study or at least 24 semester hours in subjects directly related to the position."[40] The use of these existing codes does allow CAM practitioners to be hired. In the case of the VA, this requires only the writing of a position description at the local VA level. However, it will take the creation of new OPM codes for the CAM professions to be recognized. The VA Central Office is now going through the process of getting a new OPM code for licensed acupuncturists, and this involves creating a Qualification Standard, which outlines education and licensure requirements, duties, required knowledge and skill sets, and pay scales for different levels of training and experience. Note that although both the DoD and the VA require that CAM providers be licensed, in the interest of personnel transportability, they do not require the license to be from the state in which the provider will be practicing.

Regulatory Practice Constraints

State and federal laws, often directed at consumer protection, may designate business relationships, including ownership of or financial interest in related businesses and employer-employee relationships. Such laws vary by jurisdiction and may be found in business, health care, or provider scope of practice statutes and administrative rules. For example, states may have laws that regulate whether a physician or physicians group may own or have a financial

---

[38] Office of Personnel Management. *Classification and Qualifications: General Schedule Qualifications Standards: General Health Science Series, 0601*, 2015b.

[39] Office of Personnel Management. *Classification and Qualifications: General Schedule Qualifications Standards: Health Aid and Technician Series, 0640*, 2015a.

[40] OPM, 2015.

relationship in a laboratory or MRI center to which they refer their patients. Here the law is intended to protect consumers from the physician having an interest in overutilization of these services and from this captive referral system limiting competition and increasing service costs. These laws may also delineate employees and credentials, again to protect the consumer from unlicensed providers. One category of laws here are those collectively considered part of the Corporate Practice of Medicine (CPOM) Doctrine. This doctrine was developed by the American Medical Association at the end of the last century to stem the involvement of corporations (at that time railroad, mining, and timber companies) in the practice of medicine and to prevent the commercial exploitation of physicians—i.e., corporations hiring physicians and dictating care, or padding professional charges for profit, then charging patients higher fees when the lay corporations themselves were not licensed to practice medicine.[41] The CPOM also served one additional function: CPOM laws were used to help distinguish medical doctors from "irregulars" who did not have a standard medical education.[42] Under the CPOM doctrine, only a "regular physician" could practice with other regular physicians and not irregular providers. The doctrine has come under fire, however, starting with the enactment of the Health Maintenance Organization (HMO) Act of 1973, followed by action from the Federal Trade Commission in 1979. This hasn't, however, completely eliminated its effects. Roughly 30 to 37 states still maintain a CPOM Doctrine of one sort or another.[43] In a handful of states—California, Colorado, New York, South Dakota, and Wisconsin—the doctrine is statutorily based.[44] Other states invent a CPOM policy out of a variety of state rules and regulations, including state medical licensing laws, attorney general opinions, and/or case law—and in most of these states, the CPOM Doctrine is enforced selectively. For example, Washington state law creates obstacles to medical physicians being employed by a chiropractor. Similarly, New York state law and Texas regulations preclude doctors of chiropractic from having direct ownership interests in medical practices. Although examples of various workarounds can be found, solutions are not straightforward. Such laws and regulations can be difficult to identify, and changing them may entail litigation, legislative changes, and broad stakeholder support. Interests of consumers, trade associations, suppliers, and financers may be difficult to align, and politics, along with bureaucratic inertia, frequently must be overcome in order to change the status quo.

---

[41] N. Huberfeld, "Be Not Afraid of Change: Time to Eliminate the Corporate Practice of Medicine Doctrine," *Health Matrix*, Vol. 14, 2004, p. 243.

[42] J. F. Chase-Lubitz, "Corporate Practice of Medicine Doctrine: An Anachronism in the Modern Health Care Industry," *Vanderbilt Law Review*, Vol. 40, 1987, pp. 445–448.

[43] M. H. Michal, M. S. Pekarske, M. K. McManus, and R. Van Deuren, *Corporate Practice of Medicine Doctrine: 50 State Survey Summary*, Madison, Wis.: Center to Advance Palliative Care and National Hospice and Palliative Care Organization, 2006.

[44] Michal et al., 2006.

Professional Liability Factors

Malpractice coverage, including minimum dollar limits, may be mandated in professional practice laws and insurance participation contracts. Coverage varies by jurisdiction and profession and may become problematic when requirements, experience, and expectations of professional liability carriers, as well as legal and institutional administrative practices, confront bringing on new provider types. Typically, the less-invasive practices associated with most CAM evaluation and intervention approaches are associated with comparatively lower professional liability/malpractice insurance premiums. However, when a CAM practitioner joins a conventional medical group, CAM professional liability carriers may have concerns with "deep-pocket" legal strategies that can pull multiple providers into litigation, even if their services were not contributory; thus, increasing premium costs for the CAM provider. Further, higher cost liability experience in conventional and hospital settings may require that CAM providers procure substantially higher coverage limits. These practicalities, when superimposed on limited reimbursement for many CAM services, can be a disincentive for establishment of fully integrated CAM/conventional practices.

Academic and Residency Financial Assistance

Substantial funding is given to other types of health care providers to support education and residency programs. This funding allows more practitioners to enter the workforce, because more will be able to afford their training, and the funding for residency programs ensures a better-trained workforce. Funding for the educational loan repayment and residency training of CAM providers is limited. Medical education loan repayment programs are offered to some health care providers for agreeing to practice in areas with medically underserved populations. The Indian Health Service Loan Repayment Program[45] offers loan repayment assistance to any U.S. citizen with a health profession degree and a valid license to practice who is committed to practicing at an Indian health facility. However, the larger loan repayment program offered by the National Health Service Corps[46] to those who agree to practice in a medically underserved area is offered only to practitioners covered by Medicare. Funding for residencies is usually included in appropriations for Medicare and, therefore, also open only to practitioners covered by Medicare.

---

[45] Indian Health Service, *Loan Repayment Program: Eligibility/Selection Criteria*, 2015.

[46] National Health Service Corps, *Loan Repayment Program*, 2015.

5. CAM Expert Panel

As discussed above, the first component of this project was the development of a briefing report generally containing the information shown in the previous chapters. It was prepared with the intention of providing a starting place for discussion with the panel. The second component of this project involved assembling a panel of 12 CAM providers who are experts and leaders in their professions and bringing them together for an all-day panel meeting on October 24, 2014, at RAND's offices in Santa Monica, California. For this panel each member was asked (and all panelists agreed) to step away from representing the specific organizations to which they belong and instead represent the perspective of their type of CAM provider and that relationship with policy—e.g., the relationship between state statutes, research, guidelines, and health care coverage and their type of CAM. Short biographies of each CAM expert panelist can be found in Appendix A.

In advance of the panel meeting the briefing report (discussed earlier) was sent to the panelists for their comments. Those comments have been incorporated where appropriate. In general the panelists offered more detail on a number of the topics presented in the briefing paper and added almost all the information in the *Workforce Issues* section.

The plan for the panel meeting was to begin with a review and broadening of the issues and implications laid out in the briefing paper and added through comments. The goal of the first half of the day was to cast a wide net and to be as inclusive as possible across issues that may have been missed by the briefing paper. In the afternoon the plan was then to focus on (1) prioritizing the list of issues generated to determine the most important to be presented to the policymaker panel and (2) preliminary exploration of potential next steps to mitigate negative consequences (and to promote positive ones) of the issues identified.

On the day of the meeting and after reviewing our planned agenda, the CAM panelists reframed and broadened the meeting's topic from that of profession versus procedure to what changes would be needed (including barriers to overcome) for CAM practitioners to be able to practice at the top of their ability/training. Although this frames the issue slightly differently, to practice to the full extent of their educational scope (ability/training) does mean practicing the full scope of their profession. What this panel wanted to focus on was strategies for confronting this issue.

The discussion started with acknowledging the churn now happening in the health care system—i.e., the changes in motion, and the recognition of problems with the current system that allowed those changes and/or that were revealed by the changes. The panel then went on to identify areas of need in the system (i.e., opportunities: places where the case for CAM could be made), and to choose one or two (or a few) of them to target with specific strategies. The panel's response was that the solution might be to utilize the needs not being met in the health delivery system as an opportunity for the CAM professions to offer a broader-based contribution. In essence, the panel agreed with the issues as laid out in the briefing paper but chose to focus on what the CAM groups could do to change the situation. The strategy chosen was not a political one (such as changing the statutes and trying to get legislative intent implemented), but a strategy of "expansion of scope through demonstrated service" in areas of urgent need.

Barriers to Full-Scope, Full-Training Practice

In this section we review the barriers to full-scope practice for CAM providers, as identified by the CAM panelists.

Reimbursement

Several issues were raised about whether and how CAM practitioners are reimbursed in the current health care system, and whether CAM practitioners were being considered in the various demonstration projects across the country testing alternative payment methods. The point was made that reimbursement largely determines patient access.

E&M Codes

E&M CPT codes are designed to cover services such as history taking and physical exam, patient education/guidance/counseling, the ordering of diagnostic/imaging studies, and the development of a treatment plan. They represent the ability of a provider to be reimbursed for much of the work that goes into providing primary care to patients. At present, CAM providers are not always allowed to use these codes. There is evidence that, for example, spinal manipulation combined with activity and psychosocial components yields better outcomes. See, for example, the results of the UK BEAM trial.[47] Lack of access to E&M codes discourages the addition of these components and the likelihood of better care.

Profession-Specific CPT Codes

When chiropractors first negotiated for inclusion in Medicare, they established CPT codes defined as spinal manipulation provided by a chiropractor—chiropractic manipulation treatment, or CMT. This allowed chiropractors to be covered for their services, but now if health plans are going to modify payment for spinal manipulation, which is also covered under a more general manual therapy code (97140), they must do so for separate CPT codes by provider type.

---

[47] UK Beam Trial Team, "United Kingdom Back Pain Exercise and Manipulation (UK BEAM) Randomised Trial: Effectiveness of Physical Treatments for Back Pain in Primary Care," *British Medical Journal*, Vol. 329, No. 7479, 2004, p. 1377–1384.

Treatments Without CPT Codes

There are a number of treatments offered, particularly by acupuncturists and doctors of Oriental medicine, that have shown effectiveness but for which no separate CPT code exists. Either the code for procedures such as acupuncture should be expanded, or separate codes should be developed for other procedures such as acupressure.

Limitations on Number of Visits or Total Costs, and the Need for Prior Authorization

Many health plans impose limitations either on the number of visits a member may have with a provider or on the total dollar cost of that treatment. Limitations on the number of visits tend to be set rather arbitrarily and disregard the severity of the condition and the likely healing trajectory. Limitations on the dollar costs across treatment constrain the practitioners' ability to choose between diagnostic tests and treatment. The need for prior authorization places an additional step and costs between the patient and his or her preferred mode of treatment.

Reimbursement Does Not Match the Work Done

As discussed earlier, CAM practitioners spend a substantial portion of their time educating, counseling, and listening to their patients. This type of interaction is essential to aid patients in making healthy lifestyle changes. If one goal of the health care system is to encourage these changes, then the reimbursement offered to practitioners offering this support should be reconsidered, since at present it is insufficient.

Exclusion from Design of Future Reimbursement Schemes

Going forward, the CAM professions need to sit at the table where future reimbursement schemes are being designed and step up to be included in demonstration projects for these schemes.

Licensure

State licensure laws determine the scope of practice allowed in a state for any health care profession. Doctors of Chiropractic are licensed in 50 states, the District of Columbia, and all U.S. territories. However, the other licensed CAM professions are not licensed in all states, and the scope of practice allowed in each state can vary substantially. Naturopathic doctors are licensed in 17 states, the District of Columbia, Puerto Rico, and the Virgin Islands. Acupuncturists and/or doctors of Oriental medicine are licensed, certified, or registered in 44 states and the District of Columbia. Massage therapists are licensed or certified in 44 states and the District of Columbia.

Variations in Licensure and Scope of Practice

The variations seen in licensure and scope of practice across the country hinder national efforts for the inclusion of CAM practitioners. Often the national efforts end up aimed at the lowest common denominator in terms of scope of practice for a profession.

Resistance to Increased Licensure and Scope of Practice

When the various CAM professions approach each state's legislators to institute licensure or an increase in scope of practice, they often face strong resistance from conventional medical practitioners and/or other CAM professions. In both cases, the opposing groups see any increase in privileges given to the CAM profession in question as an erosion of their rights, privileges, scope of practice, and patient base.

Regulatory (Business Practice) Barriers Can Affect Who Can Practice with Whom

CPOM Doctrine was originally meant to prevent the commercial exploitation of physicians—e.g., corporations hiring physicians and padding professional charges for profit, then charging patients higher fees even though the lay corporations themselves were not licensed to practice medicine. The CPOM Doctrine was also used to distinguish conventionally trained medical doctors from irregulars—those who did not obtain a traditional medical education. Under the CPOM Doctrine regular physicians could practice only with other regular physicians, not with irregulars. In some versions of the laws under this doctrine, the CAM professions are considered irregulars.

Business Case for CAM

Unless a business case can be made for health care systems to include CAM services, there may be no incentives, or even disincentives, for including such services. In addition, if a CAM provider can do something for lower cost, the regulators may find that attractive. However, the business entity likely will have no interest in lowering its pharmacy, imaging, and physical therapy revenue streams. Another nuance is duplicative service. If the existing system has already invested in a family doctor, physical therapy unit, and imaging suite, bringing in a chiropractor who does all three things may seem redundant. An edge for chiropractors might be to "market" their service as being a subspecialty service focusing on musculoskeletal conditions, an area of care with which conventional providers are often not as comfortable. The angle could be reducing burden on an overworked primary care practitioner resource already stretched thin with improving care for diabetes and cardiovascular patients. They key point here is that non–regulatory/policy factors may be among the most important to address. Strategically, CAM needs to identify, develop, and market where its services might seamlessly fit into existing systems and make a business case for their inclusion.

Limited Institutional Experience with Integrative Models for Both CAM and Conventional Practitioners

Although the concept of integrative medicine has been around for over a decade, there is still little information available on how to make this integration work.[48]

Few Successful Models of Integration

There are few, if any, successful business models of integrative care. A number of integrative medicine clinics and programs have been developed, but few survive their philanthropy-supported stage.[49] In fact, it is likely that most "integration" is still happening at the patient level—i.e., patients seek care on their own from a variety of practitioners.

Conventional Practitioners Often Do Not Know When and to Whom to Refer

Although a number of medical schools now offer training in integrative medicine, most practitioners still don't know enough about CAM to understand its benefits and safety for different conditions. In addition, if a conventional practitioner has a patient who might benefit from CAM, the physician doesn't know the identity or even the qualities of a good practitioner to refer to who offers that type of care.[50]

CAM practitioners do not always know how to navigate the larger health care system

Partially because of being trained outside of the larger health care system—e.g., no or few hospital residencies—most CAM practitioners do not know enough about how the health care system works to navigate it successfully. This has impacts both on connecting with referral systems and on understanding where they might fit in and provide benefit.

Broader Education About and Promotion of CAM

In addition to conventional practitioners, patients, who increasingly direct their own health care, do not always know when they would benefit from CAM treatment. The CAM community could do more to promote CAM practitioners as effective providers for conditions such as chronic pain and wellness, and as relief for the primary care workforce shortage.

---

[48] H. Boon, M. Verhoef, D. O'Hara, B. Findlay, and N. Majid, "Integrative Healthcare: Arriving at a Working Definition," *Alternative Therapies in Health and Medicine*, Vol. 10, No. 5, 2004, p. 48–56.

[49] I. D. Coulter, R. Khorsan, C. Crawford, and A.-F. Hsiao, "Integrative Health Care Under Review: An Emerging Field, *Journal of Manipulative and Physiological Therapeutics*, Vol. 33, No. 9, 2010, pp. 690–710.

[50] I. D. Coulter, B. B. Singh, D. Riley, and C. Der-Martirosian, "Interprofessional Referral Patterns in an Integrated Medical System," *Journal of Manipulative and Physiological Therapeutics*, Vol. 28, No. 3, 2005, pp. 170–174.

CAM Practitioner Training in Best Practices

If CAM practitioners are going to promote themselves as primary care, chronic pain, and wellness providers, CAM training must be enhanced to ensure that these practitioners use best practices in these areas.

Research

The funding offered by various agencies for particular interventions and research methods also affects the ability of CAM professions to be recognized for their full scope of practice.

Types of Studies Funded

Most medical research is focused on the efficacy of a particular treatment. For studies in CAM, this is the efficacy of an acupuncture treatment using particular points, or of spinal manipulation following particular protocols. To understand the impact of CAM practitioners providing broader-based care, we need comparative effectiveness studies of patient management by a doctor of chiropractic or a naturopathic doctor versus a traditionally trained medical doctor. We also need studies that examine the effects and optimal mix of multidisciplinary care teams.

Longer-Term Studies Are Needed to Capture the Impact of Prevention and Wellness

As discussed earlier, many CAM professions are focused on healthful lifestyle changes and wellness. These approaches have been shown to offer both primary and secondary prevention benefits to patients under risk of or facing chronic disease.[51] The benefits of these types of interventions usually come years in the future. Therefore, research designs that allow the capture of longer-term outcomes, and funding for these types of studies, are needed.

Areas of Need (Opportunities)

As noted earlier, the panel identified areas of need in the system (i.e., opportunities: places where the case for CAM could be made). The panel felt that one path to full recognition as a profession might be to utilize the unmet needs in the health delivery system as an opportunity for the CAM professions to offer a broader-based contribution. The areas of need (opportunities) identified included:

- care for patients with chronic disease that is wellness oriented versus disease management oriented. Panelists saw need for this care especially in areas where

---

[51] R. L. Rosenthal, "Effectiveness of Altering Serum Cholesterol Levels Without Drugs, *Proceedings* (Baylor University Medical Center), Vol. 13, No. 4, 2000, p. 351–355; A. Silberman, R. Banthia, I. S. Estay, C. Kemp, J. Studley, D. Hareras, and D. Ornish, "The Effectiveness and Efficacy of an Intensive Cardiac Rehabilitation Program in 24 Sites," *American Journal of Health Promotion*, Vol. 24, No. 4, 2010, pp. 260–266; D. Vojta, J. De Sa, T. Prospect, and S. Stevens, "Effective Interventions for Stemming the Growing Crisis of Diabetes and Prediabetes: A National Payer's Perspective," *Health Affairs*, Vol. 31, No. 1, 2012, pp. 20–26.

conventional medicine is ineffective or rarely effective, where self-care is needed, and/or where conventional care is very expensive.

- care for patients with chronic pain and musculoskeletal conditions; CAM has the potential to offer safe, effective, nonaddictive, noninvasive therapies to address these conditions
- primary care. Patient management is at present fragmented and understaffed; CAM providers could offer care coordination, continuity of care, and an expanded workforce.
- lifestyle-related/caused conditions. Prevalence of such conditions indicates a need for more lifestyle-related education and interventions; CAM providers tend to include lifestyle change education in all visits.
- end of life care. As now offered, it is expensive and invasive.
- underserved populations, of which there are still many.

General Solutions

Some general solutions were also proposed to the barriers identified, taking advantage of these opportunities. These were simply noted during the meeting, with the acknowledgment that each needed substantial future work to be fully developed and put in place:

- Demonstrate that physicians and CAM practitioners do similar E&M work and meet the audit requirements for this code.
- The CAM professions should work together to develop integrative care pathways.
- Develop and utilize CAM "ambassadors" who can negotiate between professions and "speak both languages" (CAM and allopathic medicine). These ambassadors can be developed through shared clinical training, shadowing, rotations, and residency.
- Take advantage of the funding available for demonstration projects.
- Consider developing a CAM-based board certification in integrative medicine.
- Consider developing a CAM-based Back Pain Recognition Program (the original was launched/offered by the National Committee for Quality Assurance). This effort could involve education, credentials, and residency.
- Consider other quality credentialing opportunities.
- Look into developing a CAM-based Accountable Care Organization (ACO).
- The CAM professions should work together in one area under one tent and get ahead together.

6. Health Policy Decisionmaker Panel

The third component of this project involved assembling a panel of nine individuals with firsthand knowledge of how health policy decisionmakers view CAM and bringing them together for an all-day panel meeting at RAND's Santa Monica offices. Panelists were asked (and all panelists agreed) to step away from representing the specific organizations to which they belong and instead represent the perspective of decisionmakers involved with their type of policy(ies). The meeting was held on October 24, 2015. Short biographies of each health policy decision maker panelist can be found in Appendix B.

In advance of the panel meeting, a brief report generally containing the arguments put forth by the CAM panel as to why a broader use of CAM practitioners makes sense (i.e., the opportunities) was sent to the panelists for their review in preparation for the meeting. This report can be found in Appendix C. We decided not to send this panel a full report on the issues identified by the CAM panel because we wanted to see what comments they would make *de novo*.

The plan for the day was to go over the arguments made in the briefing paper for why CAM providers should be allowed to practice to the full extent of their scope of practice and then expand upon those issues and discuss barriers to this full practice in the morning. The afternoon was to be devoted to first prioritizing these issues and barriers and then coming up with potential solutions.

On the day of the meeting and after reviewing our planned agenda, the health policy decisionmaker panel reframed the meeting's topic from a focus on what would be needed to increase the scope and utilization of CAM providers to what would improve population health and achieve the triple aim—improving the patient experience of care (including quality and satisfaction); improving the health of populations; and reducing the per capita cost of health care.[52] Panelists argued for this change in focus because they felt that many types of providers were struggling to be allowed to practice to the full extent of their scope (e.g., nurses), and there was no reason why CAM providers should be treated any differently than any other type of provider.

Additional points made along this line include:

- Payers are not interested in having more types of attending doctors.
- The various CAM professions are not equivalent to each other, so they could not be discussed in aggregate.
- The goal should be what is best for the patient, not what the provider is called; how can we allow whoever can best address the needs of the patient to have access to that patient?

---

[52] Institute for Healthcare Improvement, *IHI Triple Aim Initiative,* 2015.

- New proposed models of care will have more appeal if done for the benefit of patients and the nation rather than as a CAM priority.
- It is not about the profession type; it is about who can lead patients to better care.
- Health programs need the flexibility to pay for services that they think are effective for patient care. Therefore, there is no need for the government to define the role of every single profession/modality.
- The idea of increasing the scope and utilization of CAM providers can't be sold simply as more CAM; what is needed is the flexibility to include CAM.
- Does the profession need to be identified? If it is known that acupuncture or cognitive behavioral therapy works, it is possible that no one cares who does it.

Interprofessional Multimodality Teams

The bulk of the discussion during the day was centered around the concept of care offered by interprofessional multimodality teams, also called a multimodal community-based model. The panelists noted that current treatment by either CAM or non-CAM providers is performed in siloes and, as a result, care received by patients does not necessarily address conditions in an integrative or coordinated manner—also referred to as "siloed chaos." The panel proposed the implementation of a primary care system focused on multimodal care that could include CAM. Most of the panel agreed that these types of teams make sense and could be where health care needs to go in the future. It also satisfied the general belief that, to be relevant, this project and report needed to consider the rapidly emerging future state and not reflect the old/present state.

How These Teams Might Work

A number of points were discussed regarding how these multimodal teams might work, including that neither the full team, nor even more than one member, might be needed for every patient and problem. It was recommended that these teams provide not just medical care, or care for a particular episode, but also wellness care, prevention, and support for lifetime health. The team should also, if possible, consider the social determinants of health and the health of the patient's family. True primary care is self-care. Team providers should all provide information to patients about how to care for themselves. These models already exist, and they are called integrative medicine.

Who Should Be on the Team

There were several opinions as to the composition of the multimodal team of providers. Some argued that if the incentives and goals are set correctly, each team would be created organically. Others stated that it could be population or employer specific. In terms of organization, most agreed on the following points:

- The patient is a member of the team.
- Team members should know each other and what each brings (e.g., approach, modalities) to patient care.

- Team members likely need to be licensed (or somehow credentialed) in the types of care they provide.
- CAM providers might not be able to provide primary care, because they do not have the residency experience to handle all the issues patients bring, and some don't have the ability to diagnose.
- The teams could include CAM providers, but this would be the decision of each team.
- Health coaches may be able to help.
- Team members should be included more by what they do than by their degrees.

Who Should Lead the Team

A multimodal team should be headed by a designated lead whose role and incentive would be to provide the highest level of care, as well as decrease its cost. A decision will need to be made as to who is accountable for the care provided by the team. One panelist noted that under fee for service, practitioners are not accountable; the payer is. One idea was that the leadership should depend on the situation or condition. For general primary care, a physician may be in charge of the team (but not necessarily). However, if the patient presents with a back problem, maybe a chiropractor should be in charge and the key provider.

Additional Issues That Would Need To Be Resolved

In addition to the makeup of the team and its leadership, there are a number of other issues to resolve, including

- What does care coordination and management mean? This usually requires data, and a person who pays attention. Panelists noted that for the latter there is no particular certification. There are several types of individuals who might be involved with the team but might not need licensure (e.g., health educators).
- How would billing be restructured (incentivized) so that costs do not increase? Payment incentives that create accountability and flexibility for care based on both cost and outcomes are needed.
- Integrated medical record systems that can interface with other systems are needed.

The Need for Health Literacy

The concept of health literacy came up a number of times in the panel's discussions as a barrier for the integration of CAM in the delivery of health care. Often the term health literacy is used only in terms of the patient's understanding of the health care system and his or her care. However, in the panel's discussions this term was also used in regard to providers (both CAM and non-CAM) and their understanding of the health care system and each other, and in terms of employers and other policymakers and their understanding of CAM and multimodal teams, and how they could be used in the health care system.

Patients need to be informed on the variety of providers who can treat their condition. For instance, patients could be introduced to chiropractors before one is needed so that they have a better understanding of their options for the treatment of pain. On the other hand, barriers to accessing CAM treatments (e.g., limitations imposed by insurance companies) restrict the exposure of primary care providers to alternative forms of care.

Improvement of health literacy can (and should) take several paths. For the general population, the primary and secondary education curriculum could inform individuals of their health care options and how to access appropriate care early on. Groups can also screen and certify providers and educate the public so that consumers better understand the services provided by different professionals. For both CAM and non-CAM providers, training should include lessons on how to participate in a multimodal health care team. CAM providers are not trained to work with other CAM professionals. They are trained to work on their own. In addition, interprofessional education would broaden providers' ability to refer patients to alternative treatments. It might help to locate a CAM training program in a conventional medical school.

Regulatory and Coding Issues

A number of specific regulations and coding issues currently act as obstacles and may even preclude the creation of multimodal teams that include CAM within mainstream settings. These will need to be addressed before such teams can be adopted broadly. Note that some of these also came up as comments by the CAM expert panelists on the briefing paper and in their meeting. These include the following:

- For the CAM professions to be recognized and their practitioners hired as salaried providers to practice at VA facilities, each provider type needs a Qualifications Standard and a new occupation code. The creation of a Qualifications Standard is a VA Central Office process, currently under way for licensed acupuncturists. An OPM occupation code exists for chiropractors; however, no processes have been started to create these codes for the other CAM provider types. In the meantime, some local VAs have been able to hire individual CAM providers, particularly acupuncturists, using other occupation codes. Unfortunately, this practice is not uniform, and the lower salary limit may prevent recruitment of high-quality licensed acupuncturists. In addition, it is uncertain whether these practitioners will be able to be grandfathered into the full occupational code for their profession when it becomes available.
- At present, Medicare reimburses chiropractic doctors for only three CPT codes. These codes are for chiropractic manipulative treatment for one or two, three or four, or five regions of the spine—CPT codes 98940, 98941, and 98942, respectively. Chiropractors cannot provide their services at home (the "993" codes), nor can they charge for patient evaluation and management (the "992" codes). This is due to the limitations laid out in the definition of chiropractors as physicians in the Social Security Act, which would require an act of Congress to change.
- There is a huge statutory hurdle in the ACA, where a limited number of practitioners are considered to be primary care providers. The evidence concerning what professions and professional types are primary care providers under the ACA is circumstantial at best;

39

nonetheless, the act comes as close as the federal government ever has to stating definitively that medical physicians trained in general internal medicine, family practice, and pediatrics are primary care physicians, and nurse practitioners and physician assistants practicing in primary care are primary care practitioners. This stance is similar to that taken in the 1996 IOM report on primary care.[53] Whereas doctors of chiropractic and licensed complementary and alternative medical providers are included in the definitions of the health care workforce and of health professionals in the ACA (see Section 5101, Definitions), they are listed separately from primary care providers. The ACA also seems to refer back to the Social Security Act's (SSA's) definitions of medical physicians, nurse practitioners, and physician assistants (see Section 5501 (a) (1) (x) (2)), but completely ignores the SSA's reference to chiropractors as physicians.

- The DoD adopted a fee schedule scheme (i.e., relative value units or RVUs) to capture the workload and value (hypothetical revenue-generating capacity) of its medical facilities. Under this system providers who are Provider Type 01 (e.g., physicians, dentists, chiropractors) or 02 (e.g., physician assistants, nurse practitioners, social workers, psychologists, physical therapists) record the work they do using CPT codes, and these codes have assigned to them RVUs and regionally adjusted dollar values. Provider types other than types 01 or 02 generate no RVUs from the work they perform; thus, they are considered to be a cost to the facility. And if they reduce the work of the type 01 or type 02 providers, they can also reduce the facility's RVUs. Provider type definitions and their connection to RVUs are decided in the DoD Business Rules. The Medical Expense and Performance Reporting System (MEPRS) is the DoD Business Rule system of record, and the MEPRS Management Improvement Group can recommend changes to the Business Rules. Without a change to these rules, all CAM practitioners other than chiropractors would be considered cost add-ons to military treatment facilities.

- The Congressional Budget Office (CBO) scores (i.e., puts cost estimates on) hundreds of different programs and proposals that come before Congress. Up until this year the CBO's cost estimates ignored cost offsets. For example, the cost of expanding chiropractic services in the VA included only the salary cost of the additional chiropractors, and not what could be saved in avoided surgeries. Starting this year, Congress has instructed the CBO to perform "dynamic scoring," where many more factors are taken into consideration. However, this dynamic scoring is going to be done only on very expensive and far-reaching items such as immigration or tax reform. Therefore, this remains a barrier to educating Congress on the full impact of its decisions regarding CAM.

Next Steps

The panel discussed a number of issues that need to be addressed to move the health care system to successful multimodal care that can achieve the triple aim. In addition to addressing the coding/regulatory issues described, these include the following:

---

[53] Institute of Medicine, *Primary Care: America's Health in a New Era*, Washington, D.C.: National Academies Press, 1996.

40

- Focus on employers as the group with the biggest incentive to get this right because they can affect not only their health care costs, but also their employees' health and productivity. The military has a similar incentive.
- A business plan is needed to sell the multimodal team for large employers. This plan should highlight the triple aim–relevant outcomes.
- Recruit private-sector champions (i.e., large employers) willing to test and demonstrate the effectiveness of multimodal teams.
- Conduct prospective comparative studies and/or demonstration projects to generate evidence. One focus could be to demonstrate that approaches that include CAM can be effective replacements for harmful therapies such as opioids. The issue of whether CAM is an add-on or a substitute should be addressed.
- Align benefits and incentives in insurance packages (i.e., benefit design). Proper incentives should be in place for health plans, providers, and patients. For example, if patients with back pain have to pay six times the co-pay to see a chiropractor compared to a PCP, the clear signal to them is to avoid the chiropractic provider.
- Consider bundling the payment for a particular disorder. This scheme can contain limits for where it can be used—i.e., not all of the funds can be used for invasive modality— and payment structures can be based on outcomes.
- All types of prevention (primary, secondary, and tertiary) are important goals for the multi-modal teams in their pursuit of the triple aim. A way to reimburse providers for this care, more training on how to promote prevention, and more research on effective prevention of each type are all needed.
- In addition to the other health literacy suggestions made earlier, consider a public service campaign to educate all groups on multimodal teams.
- Consider other ways to make the professions more collaborative, to reduce the fight between the guilds. Approach each other and ask: "how do we work together better?"

7. Summary and Conclusions

In this project we had the advantage of input from a broad range of experienced and intelligent thinkers. As can be seen, the issues involved are complex, and both panels have a goal of improving patients' health. Both panels also brought up a number of the same issues, although with different emphases. These issues are summarized here.

Employers Are Important

Both groups recognized that employers are a key group in shaping the future health care system. Employers have more incentive to help improve individual health than most organizations in that (1) they pay (at least partially) for the growing cost of health care, (2) they also incur costs when their workers are injured and disabled, (3) the health of their workforce affects their productivity, and (4) good health care increases worker loyalty and can reduce turnover.

It was also noted in both panels that to support CAM and multimodal teams, employers will need a good business case. This care has to be shown to be safe, effective and cost-effective.

Education and Health Literacy Are Essential

The CAM professions face a huge educational challenge. Patients need to be educated about their options for health care and how to find CAM providers. Conventional providers need to be educated about CAM and CAM providers, and visa versa. Also, CAM providers need to learn how to work with each other across professions. All providers need to learn how to work in multiprofessional multimodal teams. Finally, employers and policymakers need to be educated about CAM and its potential benefits.

CAM Professions Need to Work Together

In addition to CAM providers learning to work together across professions, the various CAM professions also must learn to work together/collaboratively toward mutual goals. Two examples of organizations offering cross-profession collaboration in CAM are discussed in Appendix D.

Federal and State Laws and Regulations Limit the Inclusion of CAM in Health Systems

This project uncovered a number of barriers to the further incorporation of the CAM professions in federal and state laws and regulations. These have been described in more detail previously, but here are some highlights:

- **Medicare and the Social Security Act.** Medicare is allowed to reimburse care only for a physician's services as defined in the Social Security Act (Section 1861). Chiropractors are included in that definition of a physician. However, they are included in the definition only for the provision of chiropractic manipulative treatment of the spine, and although the Affordable Care Act refers to the physician definition in the Social Security Act when describing primary care, it does not refer to the section covering chiropractors. Medicare coverage seems to be the basis for many other health-related policies—e.g., coverage under some state Medicaid systems, VHA reimbursement for outside care, medical education loan repayment programs, and residency funding. For other provider types to be covered by Medicare, and for there to be broader coverage, the Social Security Act would have to be changed (by an act of Congress). Steps could also be taken to separate these other policies from Medicare.
- **Hiring at the VA and possibly the DoD.** In order to hire licensed acupuncturists, naturopaths, and massage therapists as salaried providers to practice at Veterans Health Administration facilities, VA Central Office needs to create new qualification standards and occupation codes. This will ease the process of hiring these CAM practitioners as members of their professions at the VA, and since the DoD also uses these occupation codes, it may also ease hiring there.
- **Relative Value Units.** To be counted favorably in the DoD's military health system, health care providers need to be seen as generating relative value units (RVUs). Right now providers who are Provider Type 01 (e.g., physicians, dentists, chiropractors) or 02 (e.g., physician assistants, nurse practitioners, social workers, psychologists, physical therapists) can generate RVUs. The DoD business rules would have to change for other CAM practitioners to be included in these Provider Types.
- **The Affordable Care Act and primary care.** The ACA identifies a limited number of practitioners as primary care providers. Doctors of chiropractic and licensed complementary and alternative medical providers are included in the definitions of the health care workforce and of health professionals in the ACA (see Section 5101, Definitions). However, they are listed separately from primary care providers, though there is no specific prohibition of CAM providers for primary care.
- **Congressional Budget Office scoring.** The Congressional Budget Office (CBO) scores (i.e., puts cost estimates on) programs and proposals before Congress. Up until this year the CBO's cost estimates ignored cost offsets, which makes an increase in the numbers of any type of practitioner look like a cost add-on even if it generates cost savings. Proposals before Congress regarding CAM should ask instead for "dynamic scoring," where more factors are taken into consideration, or plan to provide other evidence of potential cost savings.

- **Business relationship regulations.** The various state and federal laws that designate allowed business relationships, including ownership of or financial interest in related businesses and employer-employee relationships, need to be identified and addressed.
- **Malpractice coverage.** Barriers due to dramatically increased malpractice coverage costs for CAM providers caused by joining a conventional medical practice (i.e., creating an integrative medicine practice) should be identified and addressed.

Conclusion

As noted in this report, what began as a somewhat simple task—identify the issues related to full professional recognition versus modality recognition only—turned out to be a complex endeavor that has a wide range of policy implications. A wide range of stakeholders and social institutions would need to be involved in making policy changes. This adds considerably to the complexity surrounding any attempt to create solutions. Given the number of vested interests at play here, perhaps the single driving force should be what is best for the patient and for health care delivery to the population. Historically, each CAM profession has had to struggle alone to achieve its professional status; an approach that reinforces professional siloes. In this respect the CAM professions face challenges that were true for all the health care professions. But the process can be a lengthy one. It took chiropractors close to 100 years to achieve their present level of recognition. Such a lengthy endeavor is in the interest of neither the patients nor the health delivery system. Furthermore, across the full spectrum of health care services, the silo approach is slowly being revamped. Appropriate care ultimately should mean getting the right care for the right person at the right time, for the right problem, from the right provider, in a safe and cost-efficient manner. Where currently that might mean the appropriate care should be from a CAM provider, the current policies work against that outcome.

Appendix A. Members of the CAM Expert Panel

David Canzone, DOM, is a Doctor of Oriental Medicine licensed in New Mexico. Currently, he serves as vice chair on the board of commissioners of the National Certification Commission for Acupuncture and Oriental Medicine (NCCAOM). He was appointed by Governor Gary Johnson to the New Mexico Board of Acupuncture and Oriental Medicine and served from 1996 to 2003, finishing service as board chair. He has served on various task forces for health policy under the two subsequent governors. In 1996 Dr. Canzone worked with St. Vincent's regional hospital to create credentialing for DOMs as medical staff associates. He assisted in writing standards for credentialing, clinical pathways, and scope of practice for Oriental medicine in the hospital. He designed and managed an oncology program integrating acupuncture and Oriental medicine at New Mexico Cancer Care Associates, Santa Fe, from 1998 to 2002. From this relationship, a freestanding integrative medicine center was created to treat and educate oncology patients and their families. On a national level Dr. Canzone has served on various committees for regulation and licensing, certification and policy. He has been active in lobbying efforts in New Mexico to help establish one of the most comprehensive scopes of practice for AOM in the country. Dr. Canzone has been in private practice since 1989 in Santa Fe,. He works with his wife, Sandra Canzone, DOM. The clinic has three DOMs and a massage therapist. A subspecialty of the clinic is the treatment of oncology patients to mitigate the side effects of conventional therapies. Sandra Canzone is the cocreator of the Peregrine Institute, a 300-hour certification program in oncology massage.

Christine Goertz, DC, Ph.D., received her Doctor of Chiropractic degree from Northwestern Health Sciences University and her Ph.D. in Health Services Research, Policy and Administration from the University of Minnesota and completed a AHRQ/NIH-funded postdoctoral fellowship at the University of Minnesota. She then spent three years as a Program Officer at the National Center for Complementary and Alternative Medicine (NCCAM), National Institutes of Health (NIH), managing a $50-million portfolio focused primarily on musculoskeletal disorders. She is now the vice chancellor of research and health policy at Palmer College of Chiropractic. Dr. Goertz has been involved in the investigation of complementary and alternative medicine in military populations for more than ten years. She served as a research consultant to Birch and Davis, Inc., becoming a member of the study team for the Department of Defense Chiropractic Health Care Demonstration Project in 1997. She later joined the Samueli Institute, spending four years as an independent scientist and in research administration positions of increasing responsibility focused on the study of CAM in the military. She has also been an adjunct assistant professor of preventive medicine and biometrics at the Uniformed Services University of the Health Sciences, Bethesda, Maryland, since 2004. During her tenure at the Samueli Institute, Dr. Goertz was principal investigator on a multimillion-dollar cooperative agreement to evaluate the use of dietary supplements in the military, PI on a Department of Defense grant to conduct clinical trial pilots on the use of CAM in the military using the Practice Outcomes Development System (PODS), and co-PI of a center grant to study integrative medicine in the military (CRIMM). Relevant accomplishments include the addition of questions relative to CAM and dietary supplement use to the 2005 DoD-wide Health Related Behaviors Survey and the successful conduct of a randomized controlled clinical trial to evaluate acupuncture for acute pain in the emergency room at Andrews Air Force Base. Since joining Palmer College of Chiropractic in 2007, Dr. Goertz has completed a survey of chiropractic practice characteristics in the VA, a survey of chiropractic practice characteristics in the DoD, and a randomized controlled clinical trial evaluating the effectiveness of chiropractic care in enlisted military personnel at Fort Bliss in El Paso.

Janet R. Kahn, Ph.D., LMT, is a medical sociologist, massage therapist, and somatic awareness trainer. She is a research assistant professor in the Department of Psychiatry at the University of Vermont College of Medicine, senior policy adviser to the Consortium of Academic Health Centers of Integrative Medicine (CAHCIM), and co-principal investigator for the integrative project Mission Reconnect: Promoting Resilience and Reintegration of Post-Deployment Veterans and Their Families. She is also a presidential appointee to the federal Advisory Group on Prevention, Health Promotion and Integrative and Public Health. Previous appointments include executive director of the Integrated Healthcare Policy Consortium (2005–2011), research director of the Massage Therapy Research Consortium (2003–2008), president of the Massage Therapy Foundation (1993–2000), and research scientist at American Institutes for Research (AIR) (1977–1985). Dr. Kahn holds a B.A. in Psychology from Antioch College, an Ed.M. in Administration, Planning and Social Policy from Harvard Graduate School of Education, and a Ph.D. in Sociology from Brandeis University.

Karl C. Kranz, DC, JD, received his DC Degree at Palmer College of Chiropractic (1981), summa cum laude. He is licensed to practice chiropractic in New York, Virginia, and the District of Columbia. Dr. Kranz practiced in Virginia and served on the staff of both the American Chiropractic Association and International Chiropractors Association. He received his JD degree at the State University of New York at Buffalo (2001), cum laude, Certificate in Health Care Law. He was admitted to the bar to practice law in New York, Massachusetts, and the District of Columbia. He is the former chair of the American Public Health Association (APHA) chiropractic Special Primary Interest Group (SPIG) (prior to chiropractic achieving APHA Chiropractic Section status). Dr. Kranz is a New York State–certified firefighter and emergency medical technician (EMT). He served as the executive director of the New York State Chiropractic Association for the past 26 years and as staff and general counsel to the association as well for the past 14 years. Dr. Kranz also serves as general counsel for a number of for-profit and not-for-profit entities.

Mark McKenzie, Ms.O.M., L.Ac., is the executive director of the Accreditation Commission for Acupuncture and Oriental Medicine (www.acaom.org), the national accrediting agency recognized by the U.S. Department of Education for the accreditation of programs in acupuncture and in Oriental medicine throughout the United States. Mr. McKenzie served as dean at the College of Acupuncture and Oriental Medicine, Northwestern Health Sciences University in Bloomington, Minnesota, for over ten years and is currently on the board of directors of the Academic Consortium for Complementary and Alternative Health Care.

Dr. Bruce Milliman, ND, is a 1982 graduate of Bastyr University's Naturopathic Medicine Program. He is past president of the Washington Association of Naturopathic Physicians (WANP) and past clinical director at Bastyr University, where he has been ranked an associate professor. He was Physician of the Year (1996) of the American Association of Naturopathic Physicians (AANP). He has worked extensively to help gain access for both patients and practitioners to health insurance reimbursement for primary care naturopathic and other nonconventional services. He currently represents the AANP on the AMA CPT Editorial Panel/HCPAC (Health Care Professional Advisory Committee). He is a past AANP board member and speaker of the AANP House of Delegates. He is the founding and current president of the NAPCP. He has been a naturopathic primary care physician for 32 years, now at one of the earliest integrative clinics established in the United States, Seattle Healing Arts Center, with nearly 60 other clinicians.

Robert D. Mootz, DC, is the associate medical director for chiropractic at the Washington State Department of Labor and Industries. His position involves policy development and quality oversight regarding care of occupationally injured workers. He continues to be directly involved in development and implementation of evidence-informed decisionmaking strategies for governmental policy. His current research seeks to identify and implement improvements in the use of occupational health best practices by providers in order to improve disability prevention at a communitywide level. Additionally, Dr. Mootz has served as editor and on the editorial board of numerous chiropractic research and practice journals and is a coeditor and contributing author of numerous texts including *Chiropractic Care of Special Populations* and *Best Practices in Clinical Chiropractic*. He coedited the U.S. Department of Health and Human Services Agency for Health Care Policy and Research monograph *Chiropractic in the United States—Training, Practice and Research*, as well as the *Washington State Report on Issues in Coverage for Complementary and Alternative Medicine Services*. Dr. Mootz has served in faculty and leadership roles in many interdisciplinary organizations, including the Institute for Healthcare Improvement, American Public Health Association, and American Back Society. He is also involved in postgraduate chiropractic education, lecturing on the subjects of orthopedics, quality improvement, outcomes management, and evidence-based practice. In addition to 13 years in private practice, Dr. Mootz also served as a professor at Palmer College of Chiropractic West.

Laura E. Ocker, L.Ac., MAcOM, is in private practice in Milwaukie, Oregon (just outside of Portland). She is the president emeritus of the Oregon Association of Acupuncture and Oriental Medicine and has been a champion for greater inclusion of AOM under state health care delivery systems. Prior to opening her private practice in 2009, she worked for two Federally

Qualified Health Centers in Oregon, allowing her to practice in diverse clinical settings, including integrated primary care and OB clinics and clinics serving people recovering from drug and alcohol addiction. She currently serves on two committees of the Oregon Health Authority: the Integrative Medicine Advisory Group and the Values Based Benefits Subcommittee of the Health Evidence Review Commission. She is a 2003 graduate of the Oregon College of Oriental Medicine.

Rosa N. Schnyer is a Doctor of Acupuncture and Oriental Medicine (DAOM) and clinical assistant professor in the College of Nursing at the University of Texas, Austin, as well as adjunct faculty at the Oregon College of Oriental Medicine (OCOM) DAOM program, and the AOMA School of Integrative Medicine DAOM program. She serves as research consultant to Stanford University and the New England School of Acupuncture, and is past copresident of the Society for Acupuncture Research. A practitioner for almost 30 years and leader in the field of acupuncture research, she explores innovative research methodologies that better reflect clinical practice and evaluates acupuncture in the treatment of depression, stress-related disorders, and women's health. She maintains a private practice in Austin.

Dr. Michael Traub obtained his undergraduate degree in biological sciences from the University of California, Irvine, in 1976, where he conducted neurobiology research on learning and memory for Professor James L. McGaugh. He graduated from the National College of Naturopathic Medicine in 1981 and completed a residency there in Family Practice and Homeopathy. He became board certified in homeopathic medicine by the Homeopathic Academy of Naturopathic Physicians in 1989. Dr. Traub was recognized for his many years of service to the American Association of Naturopathic Physicians, including as president from 2001 to 2003, when he was honored with the 2006 Physician of the Year Award. He has long been active in integrative health care policy and legislative work in Hawaii and on the national level, and has served as a board member of the Integrative Healthcare Policy Consortium since 2001. He was coauthor of the *Final Report of the National Policy Dialogue to Advance Integrated Health Care: Finding Common Ground, 2001–2002* and *The Affordable Care Act and Beyond: A Stakeholder's Conference on Integrated Health Care Reform, 2010*. His father was a dermatologist, and this inspired Dr. Traub to undertake extra study in this subject. He has taught dermatology at five of the seven accredited naturopathic medical schools in North America and is the author of *Essentials of Dermatologic Diagnosis and Integrative Therapeutics*. He is a recognized authority on dermatology within the naturopathic profession. He serves on the scientific advisory boards of several natural product companies and has been actively engaged in clinical research for most of his career. Dr. Traub has been medical director of Lokahi Health Center in Kailua Kona, Hawaii, for the past 29 years. He is also board certified in naturopathic oncology by the American Board of Naturopathic Oncology.

Dr. Tino Villani is a 1986 graduate of New York Chiropractic College, with a B.S. in biology from Adelphi University. He earned a certification in chiropractic neurology in 1991. Dr. Villani practiced for 17 years in a number of different interdisciplinary settings. During this time he also served as chair of the State of Connecticut Board of Chiropractic Examiners and a member of the Federation of Chiropractic Licensing Boards for roughly ten years. He sat on the board of directors of the National Chiropractic Mutual Insurance Company (NCMIC) for two years. In 2003 he left that position to become the president and CEO of Triad Healthcare, a company that managed musculoskeletal benefits for commercial health plans. He recently left that position and currently consults in product development for MedSolutions, a large national managed-care company with MSK, cardiac, and radiology programs. He is also currently consulting for MOBE, a company developing programs to improve the health of patients using antiseizure medications.

Dr. Bill Walter is a naturopathic physician in Eugene, Oregon. He graduated from Bastyr University in 2009 and completed a one-year residency at the Bastyr Center for Natural Health in 2010. He splits his clinical practice between the Community Health Centers of Lane County (offering primary care at a county-run Federally Qualified Health Center, serving the Medicaid population) and his private practice, Golden Apple Healthcare (offering naturopathic primary care). He sits on the Peer Review Committee of his local Medicaid CCO and has been very active in Medicaid coverage for NDs in Oregon. He is author of the chapter "Economic Benefits of Naturopathic Medicine" in the forthcoming *Foundations of Naturopathic Medicine* textbook. He is cochair of the Scientific Affairs Committee of the American Association of Naturopathic Physicians and sits on the board of the Naturopathic Physicians Research Institute.

Appendix B. Members of the Health Policy Decisionmakers Panel

Kevin G. Berry, MD, joined the Samueli Institute in June 2012 as the vice president for research and evaluation. Dr. Berry leads a team of mixed-methods researchers exploring claims of healing, wellbeing, human performance and resilience in military populations managing dozens of projects in clinical and nonclinical settings. He presented on resilience before the Institute of Medicine committee exploring resilience in the Department of Homeland Security and addressed business leaders on resilience in veteran populations. Prior to joining the Institute he served the U.S. Air Force Medical Service Agency developing and overseeing combat casualty care research and development. Before that he served 30 years with the Navy including leadership positions as the chair of pediatrics at Naval Medical Center San Diego, head of medical operations at Bureau of Medicine and Surgery, deputy commander for clinical services at Tripler Army Medical Center, Hawaii, commanding officer of the Naval Hospital Pensacola, and as director of operations for Joint Task Force National Capital Region Medical. Dr. Berry received his B.S. in Biology from the University of Southern California, Los Angeles, and his Doctorate of Medicine degree from Georgetown University, Washington, D.C.. He completed a residency in general pediatrics at Regional Medical Center San Diego.

David Elton, DC, is senior vice president of clinical programs at Optum Physical Health in Golden Valley, Minnesota. Optum Physical Health helps people live healthier lives by optimizing the quality and affordability of the management of neuromusculoskeletal conditions. Optum Physical Health contracts with over 85,000 chiropractors, physical therapists, and occupational therapists nationally. As SVP of Clinical Programs for Optum Physical Health, Dave Elton is responsible for (1) quality improvement and measurement, (2) cost and quality transparency, (3) care pathway optimization, (4) prospective and retrospective utilization review, (5) consumer engagement, (6) credentialing, (7) audit and recovery, (8) medical/coverage policy development, (9) professional and government relations, (10) accreditation, and (11) customer relationships.

John Falardeau is the senior vice president for government relations for the American Chiropractic Association (ACA) in Arlington, Virginia. Responsible for monitoring legislation, formulating policy, and carrying out the course of action on the federal level for an organization of over 15,000 members, he is also active in the ACA political action committee. Prior to coming to ACA, he was the director of federal and state government affairs for the Rubber Manufacturers Association (RMA) in Washington, D.C. Among the issues he was most involved in were vehicle safety, tort reform, and international trade. Before joining RMA, he worked for two political Internet application firms, Aristotle and Votenet. Before that, he spent ten years as a senior assistant to two members of the House of Representatives. During his tenure on Capitol Hill, he was involved in drafting and monitoring legislation regarding health care, taxes, and foreign affairs. He was also active in several congressional campaigns. A United States Navy veteran, he holds a B.S. degree from the State University of New York, College at Brockport, and an M.A. degree from George Mason University.

Gary M. Franklin, MD, MPH has served as the medical director of the Washington State Department of Labor and Industries (L&I) from 1988 to the present and has a more than 25-year history of developing and administering workers' compensation health care policy and conducting outcomes research. He is a research professor in the Department of Environmental and Occupational Health Sciences and in the Department of Medicine (Neurology), as well as adjunct research professor in the Department of Health Services at the University of Washington (UW). He has served as director or codirector of the NIOSH-funded ERC Occupational Health Services Research training program since its inception. Dr. Franklin is also director of the Occupational Epidemiology and Health Outcomes Program at UW, the most productive program of its kind in the United States. This program houses and facilitates primary research as well as the secondary use of workers' compensation data to improve medical care and reduce the disability related to occupational injuries and illnesses. Because of his dual directorship roles, he is in a unique position to conduct meaningful policy-relevant health services research and provide leadership in this area. Dr. Franklin's research has focused on (1) evaluating a major quality improvement program within L&I to reduce worker disability and improve outcomes,[54] (2) identifying predictors of long-term disability among workers with back sprain and carpal tunnel syndrome, (3) assessing the risks associated with opiate use for chronic pain,[55] and (4) evaluating outcomes of lumbar fusion.[56] In addition, since the epidemic of opioid deaths became apparent earlier in the decade, Dr. Franklin has conducted several studies related to opioid prescribing practices, has translated this research directly back into state health care policy, and

[54] T. M. Wickizer, G. Franklin, R. Plaeger-Brockway, and R. D. Mootz, "Improving the Quality of Workers' Compensation Health Care Delivery: The Washington State Occupational Health Services Project," *Milbank Quarterly*, Vol. 79, No. 1, 2001, pp. 5–33; T. M. Wickizer, G. Franklin, J. V. Gluck, and D. Fulton-Kehoe, "Improving Quality Through Identifying Inappropriate Care: The Use of Guideline-Based Utilization Review Protocols in the Washington State Workers' Compensation System," *Journal of Occupational and Environmental Medicine*, Vol. 46, No. 3, 2004, pp. 198–204; IOM, 1996.

[55] G. M. Franklin, J. Mai, T. Wickizer, J. A. Turner, D. Fulton-Kehoe, and L. Grant, "Opioid Dosing Trends and Mortality in Washington State Workers' Compensation, 1996–2002," *American Journal of Industrial Medicine*, Vol. 48, No. 2, 2005, pp. 91–99; G. M. Franklin, "Early Opioid Prescription and Subsequent Disability Among Workers with Back Injuries: The Disability Risk Identification Study Cohort," *Spine* (Philadelphia, Pennsylvania, 1976), Vol. 33, No. 2, 2008, pp. 199–204; G. M. Franklin, "Opioid Use for Chronic Low Back Pain: A Prospective, Population-Based Study Among Injured Workers in Washington State, 2002–2005," *Clinical Journal of Pain*, Vol. 25, No. 9, 2009, pp. 743–751; R. K. Garg, D. Fulton-Kehoe, J. A. Turner, A. M. Bauer, T. Wickizer, M. D. Sullivan, and G. M. Franklin, "Changes in Opioid Prescribing for Washington Workers' Compensation Claimants After Implementation of an Opioid Dosing Guideline for Chronic Noncancer Pain: 2004 to 2010," *Journal of Pain*, Vol. 14, No. 12, 2013, pp. 1620–1628; Wickizer et al., 2004.

[56] S. Maghout-Juratli, G. M. Franklin, S. K. Mirza, T. M. Wickizer, and D. Fulton-Kehoe, "Lumbar Fusion Outcomes in Washington State Workers' Compensation," *Spine*, Vol. 31, No. 23, 2006, pp. 2715–2723; S. Maghout-Juratli, S. K. Mirza, D. Fulton-Kehoe, T. M. Wickizer, and G. M. Franklin, "Mortality After Lumbar Fusion Surgery," *Spine*, Vol. 34, No. 7, 2009, pp. 740–747; Garg et al., 2013.

is leading a statewide effort to educate physicians about best practice use of opioids for chronic noncancer pain.

Lori Knutson, RN, BSN, HNB-BC is both a clinician and health care administrator with over 25 years of dedication to the advancement of integrative health care. Ms. Knutson is founder and president of Integrative Healthcare Solutions LLC, a consulting firm that partners with individuals and organizations to develop and advance sustainable integrative health initiatives. In addition, she is senior director of health and wellness services for Touchstone Mental Health in Minneapolis, Minnesota. Ms. Knutson is the founding executive director (2002–2011) for the Penny George Institute for Health and Healing, Allina Health, Minneapolis, Minnesota, recognized as the largest and most comprehensive integrative health program in the United States. In her role with the Penny George Institute she partnered with philanthropists raising $25 million to seed operations and foster innovation. Ms. Knutson was instrumental in the infrastructure and database development that led to a $2.5 million NIH grant to study integrative pain management in the acute care setting. She is core faculty for Duke University's Integrative Health Leadership Program. Ms. Knutson has coauthored several book chapters and published peer-reviewed articles. In 2006, the American Holistic Nurses Association honored Ms. Knutson as the Holistic Nurse of the Year.

Karl C. Kranz, DC, JD, has served as the executive director of the New York State Chiropractic Association for the past 27 years and as general counsel to the association as well for the past 14 years. He is the former chair of the APHA chiropractic SPIG (before Section status). He is a New York State–certified firefighter and EMT. He also served as general counsel for a number of for-profit and not-for-profit entities.

Karen Milgate is a seasoned health care policy executive with a deep knowledge of Medicare and Medicaid policies, programs, operations, and data. She has devoted her 25-year career to identifying, developing, advocating, and implementing strategies that lead to a more value-based health care system. She was instrumental in the development of MedPAC recommendations on policies later included in legislation related to value-based purchasing, quality measurement, accountable care organizations, meaningful use of EHRs, and care coordination strategies. She has worked in both Republican and Democratic administrations as the deputy director for the Center for Strategic Planning and the director of the Office of Policy at CMS to help build the infrastructure and implement these policies, and to create data analytics to support innovative Medicare and Medicaid payment and delivery models. Since she left CMS in 2011, she has worked as an independent health policy consultant and assisted numerous organizations in identifying strategies for responding to ACA payment incentives. Her clients have included CMS, the Mitre Corporation, Leavitt Partners, Social and Scientific Systems, the American Chiropractic Association, the National Association of Certified Professional Midwives, several Quality Improvement Organizations, and the Catalyst For Payment Reform. She is also a frequent speaker on the interaction between the ACA and the integrative health care field. Ms. Milgate is a former research director for the Medicare Payment Advisory Commission and senior associate director for policy development for the American Hospital Association. She has bachelor's degrees in economics and international studies from American University and a master's degree in public policy from the University of Maryland. Her newest endeavor is plant spirit medicine, and she was certified as a practitioner in June 2013.

Hector Rodriguez, MBA, has been the industry chief technology officer and strategist for Microsoft's Health Plans and Provider Group since 2004. In 2012, he became the National Director of the U.S. Health and Life Sciences Industry Technology Unit, where he focuses on the development and deployment of Microsoft's "go to market" health care IT solutions and strategies. He is a member of Microsoft's Health and Life Sciences leadership team and frequently collaborates with internal and external organizations to advance the needs of the health care industry. His team works with health plans, providers, life sciences organizations, Health and Human Services, and industry partners and analysts to establish health care IT solutions as strategic business assets that enable them to reduce operational and medical costs, drive patient/member engagement, improve quality of care and service, and enable community health initiatives. Key solution areas include health care transformation, the extended patient journey and care continuum, HIPAA/HITECH compliance, multilanguage health care literacy, health improvement technologies and electronic medical records, patient engagement, cloud computing, business intelligence, and predictive analytics for health care. He works extensively with industry groups including WEDI-SNIP, HL/7, AHIP, HIMSS, HITRUST, and CAQH/CORE and is currently an adviser of the Samueli Institute—an organization dedicated to the science of wellness and healing. Hector began his career in 1982 as a software engineer at Bell Research Laboratories and has been in the IT business for over 30 years. Hector earned his M.B.A. focusing on management finance and entrepreneurship at Rutgers Graduate School of Management and his B.S. in computer science from Rutgers University.

Kirsten Tillisch, MD, is associate professor of medicine and director of the Mind-Body Research program in the Oppenheimer Center for Neurobiology of Stress at UCLA and is the chief of integrative medicine at the Greater Los Angeles VA. Her research focuses on increasing our understanding of brain-body interactions, with particular interest in irritable bowel syndrome (IBS). She utilizes functional and structural neuroimaging to identify disease-relevant central abnormalities in IBS, also using pharmacological and nonpharmacological interventions to identify treatment effects. She has pioneered the study of microbiome-gut-brain interactions in humans, showing the effects of probiotic administration on brain function in healthy women. Clinically, her primary interest is the use of mind-body and nonpharmacological approaches to treatment of chronic illness, in particular chronic pain.

CAM Professions Terminology Project: Briefing Paper for Health Policy Decision Maker Panel Review

Prepared for:

Health Policy Decision Maker Panelists

CAM Professions Terminology Project

NCMIC Foundation

Prepared by:

Patricia M. Herman, ND, PhD

Ian D. Coulter, PhD

May 14, 2015

Table of Contents

Preface

Among the primary contact/primary care health professions complementary and alternative medicine (CAM) practitioners are almost unique in that although legally recognized as members of professions their services are almost exclusively funded and researched as treatment modalities. Traditionally, members of a profession possess not only the skill to provide a service, but that they have been educated in the profession's systematic "body of theory" which guides the proper application of this skill.[1] Members of a profession also are assumed for the most part to regulate themselves and operate by a code of ethics, and are granted "professional authority" in that they have some say in when and under what circumstances their services are needed. Within healthcare medical doctors come the closest to operating as members of a fully empowered profession. For example, a medical act has been defined as any act carried out by a medical doctor without any restrictions with regard to education or training in that act.

In contrast, CAM practitioners lack professional authority in many areas. In practice this results in the following types of situations occurring for most types of CAM and at least in some states:

- Not being able to be reimbursed for evaluation and management or basic office visit (e.g., "99") codes;
- Needing a referral from a medical doctor for treatment to be reimbursed;
- Being reimbursed for fewer types of actions (e.g., treatments/modalities, diagnostics) even though being trained, educated and often licensed to provide other types of actions;
- Being licensed to offer fewer types of actions (e.g., treatments/modalities, diagnostics) than education and training would justify; and
- Having little if any research funding available to examine the effect of being seen by practitioners from different professions even if the treatment modality is the same.

The policy question we have been asked to consider at RAND is what are the policy ramifications, if any, attributable to recognizing a group legally as a legitimate profession while at the same time regulating, funding and researching it as a modality or group of modalities. This of course begs the question of whether this is how all professions should be regulated. However, at present this is clearly not the case.

Toward the goal of a RAND Report/white paper we conducted an earlier panel of CAM providers and/or members active in the CAM professions to ask them to delineate what they saw as the issue. This briefing paper lays out their main arguments for why CAM practitioners should be allowed to practice to the full extent of their training—i.e., as members of their professions. This second panel, a panel representing health policy makers, is being convened to get policy makers take on the importance and relevance of each of these arguments, and the barriers, if any, they see to increased use of CAM practitioners, and possible acceptable next steps to improve how CAM is practiced After we obtain input from the health policy maker panel, we will assemble the report. The RAND Report arising from this project will be available in the public domain and therefore, be accessible to all persons with an interest in this issue. Our aim is that this Report will serve as a valuable reference document to aid in thoughtful consideration of policy making in terms of CAM coverage, licensure, inclusion, and research.

We emphasis that RAND is not and will not be proposing any position on this topic, but feels that the concerns of the CAM professions are worthy of serious consideration given that a large proportion of the American public use CAM and some $37 billion, largely out of pocket funds, are paid out annually for this form of health care.

Acknowledgements

Funding for this project was generously provided by the NCMIC Foundation. The authors would like to acknowledge Reed Phillips, DC, PhD, and Claire Johnson, DC, MS, for recognizing the need for this project; and Carlos Ignacio Gutierrez, a Pardee-RAND graduate student and doctoral fellow who has been assisting during the panels and in gathering background data in support of this project.

Introduction

There are several trends underway in healthcare that make the optimal utilization of licensed complementary and alternative medicine (CAM) practitioners imperative. Each is briefly described below.

Shortage of primary care providers

Many report that there is a national shortage of primary care providers.[2-4] The 2010 Patient Protection and Affordable Care Act is estimated to increase the number of people with health insurance coverage by a total of 27 million by the year 2017.[5] In turn, the newly insured are expected to increase the need for primary care providers[3] beyond the demand already projected to be needed to cover our aging population and increasing prevalence of chronic disease.[2, 6, 7] As a result, a shortage of primary care providers is expected.[2, 4, 8]

Many of the proposed solutions to this primary care shortage involve programs and incentives to increase physician involvement in primary care.[2, 6, 9-11] Others have proposed increasing the workforce of non-physician primary care providers. So far these proposals have mainly focused on nurse practitioners and physician assistants as non-physician providers.[12-16] However, other types of non-physician providers have also been proposed.[12, 17] Licensed complementary and alternative medicine (CAM) practitioners might also help meet this demand.

Recent estimates show that there are over 100,000 licensed CAM practitioners in the US with a strong orientation toward primary care.[18] This estimate includes 72,000 Doctors of Chiropractic, 5,500 Naturopathic Doctors, 28,000 acupuncturists and Doctors of Oriental medicine, and 2,000 Direct-entry Midwives.[18, 19] Doctors of Chiropractic and Naturopathic Medicine have clearly established primary care training within the accreditation standards for their colleges.[20-22] Although this training is not stated in their educational standards, acupuncture and Oriental medicine (AOM) practitioners are defined as primary care providers in the statutes of three states: California, Florida and New Mexico.[23] However, the focus of AOM training is on the system of oriental medicine diagnosis and treatment. Direct-entry midwives, and in particular Certified Professional Midwives, consider themselves primary maternity care providers.[24]

Prevalence of preventable, lifestyle-related disease

The second trend that helps make the case for a broader use of CAM providers is the epidemic of preventable lifestyle-related disease. A number of studies have shown that the major causes of death in the US are lifestyle-related.[25-27] Education, counseling and support for patients making these changes have been shown to work,[28-30] and even to cost less than pharmaceutical-based prevention.[31] One group has coined the term Lifestyle Medicine to address these educational, counseling and support functions.[32] It also seems that a number of different types of practitioners can offer these services. A large review of one of the most well-known lifestyle interventions, the Diabetes Prevention Program, found that programs lay educators did as well as those run by clinically trained personnel.[33]

Most CAM practitioners incorporate lifestyle education, support and counseling into their visits with patients. A series of studies across CAM professions examined the practice characteristics of chiropractors, acupuncturists, massage therapists and naturopathic doctors. Chiropractors included lifestyle-related "counseling/education/self-care" in 25 percent of their visits with patients and made exercise recommendations in 10 to 20 percent of visits.[34] Acupuncturists provided dietary or nutritional counseling and exercise recommendations in about one-third of their visits.[35] Self-care recommendations (mainly water intake, body awareness, breathwork, and exercise) were made in over 80 percent of visits to massage therapists.[36] And about one-third of visits to naturopathic doctors included counseling and education on diet, exercise, and self-care.[37] This support of healthy lifestyle change also has been shown to have substantial benefits. Visits to worksite-based naturopathic doctors over a year for health promotion counselling, nutritional medicine and dietary supplementation lowered 10-year cardiovascular risk by one-third in a population of higher-risk workers[38]—a larger reduction than seen in statin drugs.[39] This intervention also lowered costs to society and the employer.[40] An integrative rehabilitation program consisting of acupuncture and self-care (including self- or spouse-administered acupressure and lifestyle modifications) for patients with clinical angina and proven myocardial infarction reduced death rates and healthcare utilization.[41, 42] A similar program of acupuncture and self-care (including acupressure, biofeedback and lifestyle modification) also reduced death rates for stroke patients.[43] "Typical" naturopathic care with its emphasis on self-care improved diabetic patient lifestyle habits and motivation as well as lowered HbA1c.[44]

Prevalence of chronic pain

A third trend that increases the need for CAM is the high prevalence of individuals with chronic pain. Almost 44 percent of US adults report chronic pain (with back pain, headache, and arthritis/joint pain most common),[45] and this prevalence is rising.[46] The Institute of Medicine's (IOM's) Committee on Advancing Pain Research, Care, and Education recommends that since chronic pain results from a "combination of biological, psychological and social factors," it often requires an interdisciplinary approach to assessment and treatment, and that the "effectiveness of pain treatments depends greatly on the strength of the clinician-patient relationship."[46]p3

The IOM report goes on to discuss CAM as one of the approaches with "special appeal" for patients with chronic pain whose evidence of effectiveness is accumulating.[46]p134 One national study showed that chiropractors treat 40% and acupuncturists treat 7% of people with chronic pain.[47] Another study based on the National Health Information Survey showed that between 41 and 47 percent of patients with painful neurological conditions (e.g., back pain with sciatica, migraines and headache) use CAM.[48] Individuals who use CAM for their chronic pain report good results. Chiropractic, massage and relaxation techniques were rated as "very helpful" among users for back or neck pain (61%, 65%, and 43%, respectively),[49] and 60 percent of those who used CAM for back pain found a "great deal" of benefit.[50] In contrast, conventional providers were rated as "very helpful" for back or neck pain by 27% of CAM users.[49]

A substantial number of systematic reviews also support the effectiveness of CAM for chronic pain. Acupuncture has shown effectiveness in patients with several types of pain. There is low to moderate-level evidence that acupuncture improves pain and stiffness in patients with fibromyalgia over no treatment or standard care.[51] Acupuncture may also reduce pain in dysmenorrhea,[52] and has good evidence of reductions in pain intensity and frequency in headache.[53] Acupuncture also has consistent evidence of being able to reduce pain in acute migraine and may be at least as effective as prophylactic drug treatment in preventing migraine, and has fewer adverse effects.[54] Finally, there is strong evidence that it improves pain and function in patients with osteoarthritis of the hip or knee,[55] moderate evidence that acupuncture reduces pain in patients with neck disorders,[56] and it may reduce pain and improve function in patients with chronic low back pain.[57]

Regarding spinal manipulation, there is high quality evidence that spinal manipulation offers chronic low back pain patients a small improvement in pain and function compared to other interventions.[58] And there is moderate-quality evidence that cervical manipulation and mobilization have similar effects and improve short-term pain, function and patient satisfaction in those with neck pain.[59]

Massage has also shown good effects for musculoskeletal conditions. It may improve pain and function in those with subacute and chronic low back pain, especially when combined with exercises and education,[60] and massage was found to have an immediate effect on pain and tenderness in patients with neck pain of mechanical origin.[61]

Finally, several systematic reviews have shown evidence of the effectiveness of various herbal compounds, which can be used by CAM practitioners, in different types of chronic pain. These include a variety of herbs including cayenne, devil's claw, and willow bark in patients with low back pain,[62] high concentration topical cayenne in chronic neuropathic pain,[63] one set of Chinese herbs for patients with chronic neck pain,[64] and another set of Chinese herbs for women with dysmenorrhea.[65]

Other benefits of CAM care

Cost-saving or cost-effective care

CAM has the potential of improving health at a reasonable cost or even with healthcare cost savings. A recent large systematic review found that across the comparisons made in the higher quality studies, 29 percent showed cost savings.[66] In addition, 89 percent of comparisons made in the higher quality cost-utility analyses (costs per quality-adjusted life-year or QALY) were less than $50,000 per QALY, a level generally accepted as being cost-effective.

Less invasive

In general CAM is considered by most as being less invasive than conventional care.[67] This characteristic seems to have an appeal to patients on its own, but could also contribute to the low levels of adverse events seen.[68-70]

Patient satisfaction

Finally, CAM tends to receive high patient satisfaction ratings.[71-74]

Input needed

The points above were raised by CAM practitioners in support of their bid to be more broadly included in the healthcare system and to be able to practice to the full extent of their training and education. Thus, these points understandably reflect their point of view. The topic is clearly important to the CAM professions but the question might be is it important anyone else? Two other groups whose opinions and perspectives should be considered are patients and policy makers. To this end, we are interested in whether from a policy point of view having CAM practitioners' services being treated as particular modalities or procedures, rather than professional services, matters.

Those who must make decisions affecting the broader healthcare system including those related to regulation, licensure, reimbursement, and workforce may see things differently than do patients or the CAM providers themselves. We ask that you do three things in response to the points raised here. First, where needed, please offer your perspective on the issues raised. Do the trends presented above favor of broader CAM use and/or a change in healthcare policies toward CAM practitioners? Second, please feel free to add additional issues or challenges to the list. And finally, we would like your input on what types of things, if any, could be done to improve the contribution of CAM to overall patient care. Does the present approach to CAM professions unnecessarily limit their members' contribution to their patients and to the health care system more generally? If so, what types of research, arguments or demonstrations would you accept as evidence to justify a broader role for CAM practitioners in the delivery of healthcare?

Thank you in advance for your thoughts on this topic and we look forward to hearing from you at our panel meeting on May 28th at RAND in Santa Monica.

References

1.   2(3):45-55, E.G., *Attributes of a Profession.* Social Work, 1957. **2**(3): p. 45-55.

2.   Bodenheimer, T. and H.H. Pham, *Primary care: current problems and proposed solutions.* Health Affairs, 2010. **29**(5): p. 799-805.

3.   Hofer, A.N., J. ABRAHAM, and I. Moscovice, *Expansion of coverage under the Patient Protection and Affordable Care Act and primary care utilization.* Milbank Quarterly, 2011. **89**(1): p. 69-89.

4.   Huang, E.S. and K. Finegold, *Seven Million Americans Live In Areas Where Demand For Primary Care May Exceed Supply By More Than 10 Percent.* Health Affairs, 2013. **32**(3): p. 614-621.

5.   Congressional Budget Office, *CBO's February 2013 Estimate of the Effects of the Affordable Care Act on Health Insurance Coverage,* 2013, Congressional Budget Office: Washington, DC.

6.   Bodenheimer, T., K. Grumbach, and R.A. Berenson, *A lifeline for primary care.* New England Journal of Medicine, 2009. **360**(26): p. 2693-2696.

7.   Colwill, J.M., J.M. Cultice, and R.L. Kruse, *Will generalist physician supply meet demands of an increasing and aging population?* Health Affairs, 2008. **27**(3): p. w232-w241.

8.   Steinwald, A.B., *Primary Care Professionals: Recent Supply Trends, Projections, and Valuation of Services,* 2008, United States Government Accountability Office: Washington, DC.

9.   Dick III, J.F., et al., *The effect of rural training experiences during residency on the selection of primary care careers: a retrospective cohort study from a single large internal medicine residency program.* Teaching and learning in medicine, 2011. **23**(1): p. 53-57.

10. Linzer, M., et al., *Working conditions in primary care: physician reactions and care quality.* Annals of internal medicine, 2009. **151**(1): p. 28-36.

11. Siegrist, J., et al., *Work stress of primary care physicians in the US, UK and German health care systems.* Social science & medicine, 2010. **71**(2): p. 298-304.

12. Donaldson, M.S., *Primary care: America's health in a new era*1996: National Academies Press.

13. Green, L.V., S. Savin, and Y. Lu, *Primary Care Physician Shortages Could Be Eliminated Through Use Of Teams, Nonphysicians, And Electronic Communication.* Health Affairs, 2013. **32**(1): p. 11-19.

14. Hooker, R.S., J.F. Cawley, and W. Leinweber, *Career flexibility of physician assistants and the potential for more primary care.* Health Affairs, 2010. **29**(5): p. 880-886.

15. Naylor, M.D. and E.T. Kurtzman, *The role of nurse practitioners in reinventing primary care.* Health Affairs, 2010. **29**(5): p. 893-899.

16. Pohl, J.M., et al., *analysis & commentary Unleashing Nurse Practitioners' Potential To Deliver Primary Care And Lead Teams.* Health Affairs, 2010. **29**(5): p. 900-905.

17. Garson, A., et al., *A New Corps Of Trained Grand-Aides Has The Potential To Extend Reach Of Primary Care Workforce And Save Money.* Health Affairs, 2012. **31**(5): p. 1016-1021.

18. Goldstein, M.S. and J. Weeks, eds. *Meeting the Nation's Primary Care Needs: Current and Prospective Roles of Doctors of Chiropractic and Naturopathic Medicine, Practitioners of Acupuncture and Oriental Medicine, and Direct-Entry Midwives.* 2013, Academic Consortium for Complementary and Alternative Health Care: Seattle, WA.

19. Goldblatt, E., et al., eds. *Clinicians and Educators Desk Reference on the Licensed Complementary and Alternative Health Care Professions.* 2nd ed. 2013, Academic Consortium for Complementary and Alternative Health Care (ACCAHC): Seattle, WA.

20. Winterstein, J.F., et al. *Chiropractic Physicians And Primary Care.* ACA News, 2012.

21. American Association of Naturopathic Physicians. *Naturopathic Physicians: Natural Medicine. Real Solutions. Professional Education.* 2014 [cited 2014 December 5]; Available from: http://www.naturopathic.org/education.

22. Fleming, S.A. and N.C. Gutknecht, *Naturopathy and the primary care practice.* Primary Care: Clinics in Office Practice, 2010. **37**(1): p. 119-136.

23. Anderson, B., et al., *Acupuncture and Oriental Medicine Practitioners and Primary Care*, in *Meeting the Nation's Primary Care Needs: Current and Prospective Roles of Doctors of Chiropractic and Naturopathic Medicine, Practitioners of Acupuncture and Oriental Medicine, and Direct-Entry Midwives*, M.S. Goldstein and J. Weeks, Editors. 2013, Academic Consortium for Complementary and Alternative Health Care: Seattle, WA. p. 23-32.

24. Myers-Ciecko, J.A., M. Hicks, and S. Myers, *Direct-Entry Midwifery and Primary Maternity Care*, in *Meeting the Nation's Primary Care Needs: Current and Prospective Roles of Doctors of Chiropractic and Naturopathic Medicine, Practitioners of Acupuncture and Oriental Medicine, and Direct-Entry Midwives*, M.S. Goldstein and J. Weeks, Editors. 2013, Academic Consortium for Complementary and Alternative Health Care: Seattle, WA. p. 49-61.

25. McGinnis, J.M. and W.H. Foege, *Actual causes of death in the United States.* Jama, 1993. **270**(18): p. 2207-2212.

26. Mokdad, A.H., et al., *Actual causes of death in the United States, 2000.* Jama, 2004. **291**(10): p. 1238-1245.

27. Danaei, G., et al., *The preventable causes of death in the United States: comparative risk assessment of dietary, lifestyle, and metabolic risk factors.* PLoS medicine, 2009. **6**(4): p. e1000058.

28. Vojta, D., et al., *Effective interventions for stemming the growing crisis of diabetes and prediabetes: a national payer's perspective.* Health Affairs, 2012. **31**(1): p. 20-26.

29. Rosenthal, R.L., *Effectiveness of altering serum cholesterol levels without drugs.* Proceedings (Baylor University. Medical Center), 2000. **13**(4): p. 351.

30. Silberman, A., et al., *The effectiveness and efficacy of an intensive cardiac rehabilitation program in 24 sites.* American Journal of Health Promotion, 2010. **24**(4): p. 260-266.

31. Herman, W.H., et al., *The cost-effectiveness of lifestyle modification or metformin in preventing type 2 diabetes in adults with impaired glucose tolerance.* Annals of internal medicine, 2005. **142**(5): p. 323-332.

32. Sagner, M., et al., *Lifestyle medicine potential for reversing a world of chronic disease epidemics: from cell to community.* International journal of clinical practice, 2014. **68**(11): p. 1289-1292.

33. Ali, M.K., J.B. Echouffo-Tcheugui, and D.F. Williamson, *How effective were lifestyle interventions in real-world settings that were modeled on the Diabetes Prevention Program?* Health Affairs, 2012. **31**(1): p. 67-75.

34. Mootz, R.D., et al., *Characteristics of chiropractic practitioners, patients, and encounters in Massachusetts and Arizona.* Journal of manipulative and physiological therapeutics, 2005. **28**(9): p. 645-653.

35. Sherman, K.J., et al., *The practice of acupuncture: who are the providers and what do they do?* The Annals of Family Medicine, 2005. **3**(2): p. 151-158.

36. Sherman, K.J., et al., *A survey of training and practice patterns of massage therapists in two US states.* BMC Complementary and Alternative Medicine, 2005. **5**(1): p. 13.

37. Boon, H.S., et al., *Practice patterns of naturopathic physicians: results from a random survey of licensed practitioners in two US States.* BMC Complementary and Alternative Medicine, 2004. **4**(1): p. 14.

38. Seely, D., et al., *Naturopathic medicine for the prevention of cardiovascular disease: a randomized clinical trial.* Canadian Medical Association Journal, 2013. **185**(9): p. E409-E416.

39. Franco, O.H., et al., *Primary prevention of cardiovascular disease: cost-effectiveness comparison.* International journal of technology assessment in health care, 2007. **23**(01): p. 71-79.

40. Herman, P.M., et al., *A naturopathic approach to the prevention of cardiovascular disease: cost-effectiveness analysis of a pragmatic multi-worksite randomized clinical trial.* Journal of Occupational and Environmental Medicine, 2014. **56**(2): p. 171.

41. Ballegaard, S., et al., *Long-term effects of integrated rehabilitation in patients with advanced angina pectoris: a nonrandomized comparative study.* Journal of Alternative & Complementary Medicine, 2004. **10**(5): p. 777-783.

42. Ballegaard, S., et al., *Addition of acupuncture and self-care education in the treatment of patients with severe angina pectoris may be cost beneficial: an open, prospective study.* The Journal of Alternative and Complementary Medicine, 1999. **5**(5): p. 405-413.

43. Magnusson, G., et al., *Long-term effects of integrated rehabilitation in patients with stroke: a nonrandomized comparative feasibility study.* The Journal of Alternative and Complementary Medicine, 2010. **16**(4): p. 369-374.

44. Bradley, R., et al., *Adjunctive naturopathic care for type 2 diabetes: patient-reported and clinical outcomes after one year.* BMC Complementary and Alternative Medicine, 2012. **12**(1): p. 44.

45. Tsang, A., et al., *Common chronic pain conditions in developed and developing countries: gender and age differences and comorbidity with depression-anxiety disorders.* The journal of pain, 2008. **9**(10): p. 883-891.

46. Institute of Medicine, *Relieving Pain in America: A Blueprint for Transforming Prevention, Care, Education, and Research* 2011, Washington, DC: National Academies Press.

47. Breuer, B., R. Cruciani, and R.K. Portenoy, *Pain management by primary care physicians, pain physicians, chiropractors, and acupuncturists: a national survey.* Southern medical journal, 2010. **103**(8): p. 738-747.

48. Wells, R.E., et al., *Complementary and alternative medicine use among US adults with common neurological conditions.* Journal of neurology, 2010. **257**(11): p. 1822-1831.

49. Wolsko, P.M., et al., *Patterns and perceptions of care for treatment of back and neck pain: results of a national survey.* Spine, 2003. **28**(3): p. 292-297.

50. Kanodia, A.K., et al., *Perceived benefit of Complementary and Alternative Medicine (CAM) for back pain: a national survey.* The Journal of the American Board of Family Medicine, 2010. **23**(3): p. 354-362.

51. Deare, J.C., et al., *Acupuncture for treating fibromyalgia.* Cochrane Database of Systermatic Reviews, 2013. **5**.

52. Smith, C.A., et al., *Acupuncture for dysmenorrhoea.* Cochrane Data Syst Rev, 2011.

53. Linde, K., et al., *Acupuncture for tension-type headache.* Cochrane Database Syst Rev, 2009. **1**(1).

54. Linde, K., et al., *Acupuncture for migraine prophylaxis.* Cochrane Database Syst Rev, 2009. **1**(1).

55. Manheimer, E., et al., *Acupuncture for peripheral joint osteoarthritis.* Cochrane Database Syst Rev, 2010. **1**.

56. Trinh, K., et al., *Acupuncture for neck disorders.* The Cochrane Library, 2007.

57. Furlan, A.D., et al., *Acupuncture and dry-needling for low back pain.* Cochrane Database Syst Rev, 2005. **1**.

58. Rubinstein, S.M., et al., *Spinal manipulative therapy for chronic low-back pain.* Cochrane Database Syst Rev, 2011. **2**(CD008112).

59. Gross, A., et al., *Manipulation or mobilisation for neck pain.* Cochrane Database Syst Rev, 2010. **1**.

60. Furlan, A.D., et al., *Massage for low-back pain.* Cochrane Database Syst Rev, 2008. **4**(4).

61. Patel, K.C., et al., *Massage for mechanical neck disorders.* Cochrane Database Syst Rev, 2012. **9**.

62. Gagnier, J.J., et al., *Herbal medicine for low back pain.* Cochrane Database Syst Rev, 2006. **2**.

63. Derry, S., et al., *Topical capsaicin (high concentration) for chronic neuropathic pain in adults.* Cochrane Database Syst Rev, 2013. **2**.

64. Cui, X., K. Trinh, and Y.J. Wang, *Chinese herbal medicine for chronic neck pain due to cervical degenerative disc disease.* Cochrane Database Syst Rev, 2010. **1**.

65. Zhu, X., et al., *Chinese herbal medicine for primary dysmenorrhoea.* Cochrane Database Syst Rev, 2008. **2**.

66. Herman, P.M., et al., *Are complementary therapies and integrative care cost-effective? A systematic review of economic evaluations.* BMJ open, 2012. **2**(5): p. e001046.

67. Swartzman, L.C., et al., *What accounts for the appeal of complementary/alternative medicine, and what makes complementary/alternative medicine "alternative"?* Medical decision making, 2002. **22**(5): p. 431-450.

68.   Rubinstein, S.M., *Adverse events following chiropractic care for subjects with neck or low-back pain: do the benefits outweigh the risks?* Journal of manipulative and physiological therapeutics, 2008. **31**(6): p. 461-464.

69.   Rubinstein, S.M., et al., *Benign adverse events following chiropractic care for neck pain are associated with worse short-term outcomes but not worse outcomes at three months.* Spine, 2008. **33**(25): p. E950-E956.

70.   MacPherson, H., et al., *Patient reports of adverse events associated with acupuncture treatment: a prospective national survey.* Quality and Safety in Health Care, 2004. **13**(5): p. 349-355.

71.   Oberg, E.B., et al., *Older adults' perspectives on naturopathic medicine's impact on healthy aging.* Explore (New York, NY), 2013. **10**(1): p. 34-43.

72.   Gaumer, G., *Factors associated with patient satisfaction with chiropractic care: survey and review of the literature.* Journal of manipulative and physiological therapeutics, 2006. **29**(6): p. 455-462.

73.   Braun, L.A., et al., *Massage therapy for cardiac surgery patients—a randomized trial.* The Journal of Thoracic and Cardiovascular Surgery, 2012. **144**(6): p. 1453-1459. e1.

74.   Thomas, K., et al., *Randomised controlled trial of a short course of traditional acupuncture compared with usual care for persistent non-specific low back pain.* Bmj, 2006. **333**(7569): p. 623.

Appendix D. Past Collective Efforts Across the CAM Professions

There are two groups that provide a collective voice for complementary and integrative medicine to policy issues. The first is the Integrative Healthcare Policy Consortium (IHPC), founded after the 2001 *National Policy Dialogue to Advance Integrated Health Care: Finding Common Ground (NPD) meeting.* IHPC is the CAM and integrative health care provider groups' single voice for policy, legislation, and regulatory issues. For example, the IHPC helped naturopathic medicine and massage therapy gain access to the CPT Editorial Panel Advisory Committee, called the Health Care Professional Advisory Committee, or HCPAC. The IHPC was also key in getting Section 2706 into the 2010 Affordable Care Act, and in 2004 it created the Academic Consortium for Complementary and Alternative Health Care (ACCAHC).

ACCAHC is the second group that provides a collective voice for complementary and alternative medicine educational/academic organizations. ACCAHC is made up of the academic institutions, accrediting agencies, and certification and testing organizations of the various complementary and alternative health care disciplines. ACCAHC worked for more than a year through a series of communications to ensure that the current National Center for Complementary and Alternative Medicine (NCCAM; now called the National Center for Complementary and Integrative Health) Strategic Plan included multiple references to CAM "disciplines" and not just to CAM modalities, interventions, approaches, practices, and products. These efforts were justified by the terminology used in the law that established NCCAM (Title VI Section 601 of the Omnibus Appropriations Act of 1999 [P.L. 105-277]). This law specifically said in Section 485D(a) that NCCAM's purpose was to conduct and support basic and applied research with "respect to identifying, investigating, and validating complementary and alternative treatment, diagnostic and prevention modalities, *disciplines and systems*"[emphasis added].

Also through suggestions from ACCAHC, on May 15, 2005, the Consortium of Academic Health Centers for Integrative Medicine (CAHCIM; a consortium of academic medical centers) modified its definition of integrative medicine from

> Integrative Medicine is the practice of medicine that reaffirms the importance of the relationship between practitioner and patient, focuses on the whole person, is informed by evidence, and makes use of all appropriate therapeutic approaches to achieve optimal health and healing.

to

> Integrative Medicine is the practice of medicine that reaffirms the importance of the relationship between practitioner and patient, focuses on the whole person, is informed by evidence, and makes use of all appropriate therapeutic approaches,

healthcare professionals and disciplines to achieve optimal health and healing [emphasis added in the referenced article][57]

[57] P. J. Benjamin, R. Phillips, D. Warren, C. Salveson, R. Hammerschlag, P. Snider, M. Haas, R. Barrett, T. Chapman, and R Kaneko "Response to a Proposal for an Integrative Medicine Curriculum," *Journal of Alternative and Complementary Medicine*, Vol. 13, No. 9, 2007, pp. 1021–1034.

References

2010 Tennessee Code, Title 63, Chapter 6, Part 2, 63-6-205, amended 2012. As of August 28, 2015:
http://law.justia.com/codes/tennessee/2010/title-63/chapter-6/part-2/63-6-205/

American Psychiatric Association, *Practice Guideline for the Treatment of Patients with Major Depressive Disorder*, 3rd ed., Arlington, Va.: American Psychiatric Association, 2010.

American Society of Anesthesiologists Task Force on Chronic Pain Management, "Practice Guidelines for Chronic Pain Management," *Anesthesiology*, Vol. 112, No. 4, 2010, pp. 1–24.

Barnes, P. M., B. Bloom, and R. L. Nahin, "Complementary and Alternative Medicine Use Among Adults and Children: United States, 2007," in *National Health Statistics Reports*, Hyattsville, Md., 2008.

Benjamin, P. J., R. Phillips, D. Warren, C. Salveson, R. Hammerschlag, P. Snider, M. Haas, R. Barrett, T. Chapman, and R Kaneko, "Response to a Proposal for an Integrative Medicine Curriculum," *Journal of Alternative and Complementary Medicine*, Vol. 13, No. 9, 2007, pp. 1021–1034.

Blum, J. D., "Non-Discrimination and the Role of Complementary and Alternative Medicine," *BNA's Health Law Reporter*, Vol., 23, 2014, pp. 1–5.

Boon, H., M. Verhoef, D. O'Hara, B. Findlay, and N. Majid, "Integrative Healthcare: Arriving at a Working Definition," *Alternative Therapies in Health and Medicine*, Vol. 10, No. 5, 2004, p. 48–56.

Chase-Lubitz, J. F., "Corporate Practice of Medicine Doctrine: An Anachronism in the Modern Health Care Industry," *Vanderbilt Law Review*, Vol. 40, 1987, pp. 445–448.

Childs, J. D., J. A. Cleland, J. M. Elliott, D. S. Teyhen, R. S. Wainner, J. M. Whitman, B. J. Sopky, J. J. Godges, T. W. Flynn, and A. Delitto, "Neck Pain: Clinical Practice Guidelines Linked to the International Classification of Functioning, Disability, and Health from the Orthopaedic Section of the American Physical Therapy Association," *Journal of Orthopedic Sports Physical Therapy*, Vol. 38, No. 9, 2008, pp. A1–A34.

Chou, R., A. Qaseem, V. Snow, D. Casey, J. T. Cross, P. Shekelle, and D. K. Owens, "Diagnosis and Treatment of Low Back Pain: A Joint Clinical Practice Guideline from the American College of Physicians and the American Pain Society," *Annals of Internal Medicine*, Vol. 147, No. 7, 2007, pp. 478–491.

Chou, R., "In the Clinic: Low Back Pain," *Annals of Internal Medicine*, 2014, pp. 1–16.

Coulter, I. D., B. B. Singh, D. Riley, and C. Der-Martirosian, "Interprofessional Referral Patterns in an Integrated Medical System," *Journal of Manipulative and Physiological Therapeutics*, Vol. 28, No. 3, 2005, pp. 170–174.

Coulter, I. D., R. Khorsan, C. Crawford, and A.-F. Hsiao, "Integrative Health Care Under Review: An Emerging Field, *Journal of Manipulative and Physiological Therapeutics*, Vol. 33, No. 9, 2010, pp. 690–710.

Dawson, K. A., L. Dawson, A. Thomas, and P. M. Tiidus, "Effectiveness of Regular Proactive Massage Therapy for Novice Recreational Runners," *Physical Therapy in Sport*, Vol. 12, No. 4, 2011, p. 182–187.

Delitto, A., S. Z. George, L. Van Dillen, J. M. Whitman, G. Sowa, P. Shekelle, T. R. Denninger, and J. J. Godges, "Low Back Pain Clinical Practice Guidelines Linked to the International Classification of Functioning, Disability, and Health," *Journal of Orthopedic Sports Physical Therapy*, Vol. 42, No. 4, 2012, pp. A1–A57.

Franklin, G. M., "Early Opioid Prescription and Subsequent Disability Among Workers with Back Injuries: The Disability Risk Identification Study Cohort," *Spine* (Philadelphia, Pennsylvania, 1976), Vol. 33, No. 2, 2008, pp. 199–204.

———, "Opioid Use for Chronic Low Back Pain: A Prospective, Population-Based Study Among Injured Workers in Washington State, 2002–2005," *Clinical Journal of Pain*, Vol. 25, No. 9, 2009, pp. 743–751.

Franklin, G. M., J. Mai, T. Wickizer, J. A. Turner, D. Fulton-Kehoe, and L. Grant, "Opioid Dosing Trends and Mortality in Washington State Workers' Compensation, 1996–2002," *American Journal of Industrial Medicine*, Vol. 48, No. 2, 2005, pp. 91–99.

Garg, R. K., D. Fulton-Kehoe, J. A. Turner, A. M. Bauer, T. Wickizer, M. D. Sullivan, and G. M. Franklin, "Changes in Opioid Prescribing for Washington Workers' Compensation Claimants After Implementation of an Opioid Dosing Guideline for Chronic Noncancer Pain: 2004 to 2010," *Journal of Pain*, Vol. 14, No. 12, 2013, pp. 1620–1628.

Gartlehner, G., R. A. Hansen, D. Nissman, D. N, Lohr, and T. S. Carey, "Criteria for Distinguishing Effectiveness from Efficacy Trials in Systematic Reviews," in *Technical Reviews*, Rockville, Md.: Agency for Healthcare Research and Quality, 2006.

Goldblatt, E., P. Snider, J. Weeks, B. Rosenthal, and S. Quinn, eds., *Clinicians' and Educators' Desk Reference on the Licensed Complementary and Alternative Healthcare Professions.* 2nd ed., Raleigh, N.C.: Lulu Enterprises, 2013.

Goldstein, M. S., and J. Weeks, eds., Meeting the Nation's Primary Care Needs: Current and Prospective Roles of Doctors of Chiropractic and Naturopathic Medicine, Practitioners of Acupuncture and Oriental Medicine, and Direct-Entry Midwives, Seattle: Academic

Consortium for Complementary and Alternative Health Care, 2013. As of August 28, 2015:
http://web.archive.org/web/20090112214025/http://www.scstatehouse.gov/code/t40c031.htm

Greenwood, E., "Attributes of a Profession," *Social Work*, Vol. 2, No. 3, 1957, pp. 45–55.

Guzman, J., D. S. Haldeman, L. J. Carroll, E. J. Carragee, E. L. Hurwitz, M. P. Peloso, M. Nordin, J. D. Cassidy, L. W. Holm, P. Cote, J. van der Velde, and S. Hogg-Johnson, "Clinical Practice Implications of the Bone and Joint Decade 2000–2010 Task Force on Neck Pain and Its Associated Disorders: From Concepts and Findings to Recommendations," *Spine*, Vol. 33, No. 45, 2008, pp. S199–S213.

Haas, M., B. Goldberg, M. Aickin, B. Ganger, and M. Attwood, "A Practice-Based Study of Patients with Acute and Chronic Low Back Pain Attending Primary Care and Chiropractic Physicians: Two-Week to 48-Month Follow-Up," *Journal of Manipulative and Physiological Therapeutics*, Vol. 27, No. 3, 2004, pp. 160–169.

Healthcare Analysis and Information Group, *2011 Complementary and Alternative Medicine Survey*, Department of Veterans Affairs, Washington, D.C.: Veterans Health Administration. 2011.

Herman, P. M., K. D'Huyvetter, and M. J. Mohler, "Are Health Services Research Methods a Match for CAM?" *Alternative Therapies in Health and Medicine*, Vol. 12, No. 3, 2006, p. 78–83.

Huberfeld, N., "Be Not Afraid of Change: Time to Eliminate the Corporate Practice of Medicine Doctrine," *Health Matrix*, Vol. 14, 2004, p. 243.

Indian Health Service, *Loan Repayment Program: Eligibility/Selection Criteria*, 2015.

Institute for Healthcare Improvement, *IHI Triple Aim Initiative,* 2015.

Institute of Medicine, *Primary Care: America's Health in a New Era*, Washington, D.C.: National Academies Press, 1996.

IOM—*See* Institute of Medicine.

Kahn, J. R., and M. B. Menard, *Massage Therapy Research Agenda: 2015 and Beyond*, Evanston, Ill.: Massage Therapy Foundation, 2014.

Kaiser Permanente, *2014 Disclosure Form for Kaiser Permanente Small Business Gold 0/30 Copayment HMO Plan*, Oakland, Calif.: Kaiser Permanente, 2014, p. 64.

Koes, B. W., M. van Tulder, C.-W. C. Lin, L. G. Macedo, J. McAuley, and C. Maher, "An Updated Overview of Clinical Guidelines for the Management of Non-Specific Low Back Pain in Primary Care," *European Spine Journal*, Vol. 19, No. 12, 2010, pp. 2075–2094.

Langevin, H. M., P. M Wayne, H. MacPherson, R. Schnyer, R. M. Milley, V. Napadow, L. Lao, J. Park, R. E. Harris, and M. Cohen, "Paradoxes in Acupuncture Research: Strategies for

Moving Forward" *Evidence-Based Complementary and Alternative Medicine, 2011*, 2011, pp. 1–11.

MacPherson, H., A. White, M. Cummings, K. A. Jobst, K. Rose, and R. C. Niemtzow, "Standards for Reporting Interventions in Controlled Trials of Acupuncture: The STRICTA Recommendations" *Journal of Alternative and Complementary Medicine*, Vol. 8, No. 1, 2002, pp. 85–89.

MacPherson, H., D. G. Altman, R. Hammerschlag, L. Youping, W. Taixiang, A. White, and D. Moher, "Revised Standards for Reporting Interventions in Clinical Trials of Acupuncture (STRICTA): Extending the CONSORT Statement," *Journal of Evidence-Based Medicine*, Vol. 3, No. 3, 2010, pp. 140–155.

Maghout-Juratli, S., G. M. Franklin, S. K. Mirza, T. M. Wickizer, and D. Fulton-Kehoe, "Lumbar Fusion Outcomes in Washington State Workers' Compensation," *Spine*, Vol. 31, No. 23, 2006, pp. 2715–2723.

Maghout-Juratli, S., S. K. Mirza, D. Fulton-Kehoe, T. M. Wickizer, and G. M. Franklin, "Mortality After Lumbar Fusion Surgery," *Spine*, Vol. 34, No. 7, 2009, pp. 740–747.

Michal, M. H., M. S. Pekarske, M. K. McManus, and R. Van Deuren, *Corporate Practice of Medicine Doctrine: 50 State Survey Summary*, Madison, Wis.: Center to Advance Palliative Care and National Hospice and Palliative Care Organization, 2006.

Mootz, R. D., I. D. Coulter, and G. D. Schultz, "Professionalism and Ethics in Chiropractic," in *Principles and Practices of Chiropractic*, S. Haldeman, ed., New York: McGraw Hill, 2005, pp. 201–219.

National Health Service Corps, *Loan Repayment Program*, 2015.

Non-Discrimination in Health Care, in *42 U.S.Code § 300gg-5.* 2010.

Office of Personnel Management. *Classification and Qualifications: General Schedule Qualifications Standards: Health Aid and Technician Series, 0640*, 2015a.

———. *Classification and Qualifications: General Schedule Qualifications Standards: General Health Science Series, 0601*, 2015b.

OPM—*See* Office of Personnel Management.

Ritenbaugh, C., M. Verhoef, S. Fleishman, H. Boon, and A. Leis, "Whole Systems Research: A Discipline for Studying Complementary and Alternative Medicine," *Alternative Therapies in Health and Medicine*, Vol. 9, No. 4, 2002, pp. 32–36.

Ritenbaugh, C., R. Hammerschlag, C. Calabrese, S. Mist, M. Aickin, E. Sutherland, J. Leben, L. DeBar, C. Elder, and S. F. Dworkin, "A Pilot Whole Systems Clinical Trial of Traditional Chinese Medicine and Naturopathic Medicine for the Treatment of Temporomandibular

Disorders," *Journal of Alternative and Complementary Medicine*, Vol. 14, No. 5, 2008, pp. 475–487.

Rosenthal, R. L., "Effectiveness of Altering Serum Cholesterol Levels Without Drugs, *Proceedings* (Baylor University Medical Center), Vol. 13, No. 4, 2000, p. 351–355.

Salhani, D., and I. D. Coulter, "The Politics of Interprofessional Working and the Struggle for Professional Autonomy in Nursing," *Social Science and Medicine*, Vol. 68, No. 7, 2009, pp. 1221–1228.

Seely, D., O. Szczurko, K. Cooley, H. Fritz, S. Aberdour, C. Herrington, P. Herman, P. Rouchotas, D. Lescheid, and R. Bradley, "Naturopathic Medicine for the Prevention of Cardiovascular Disease: A Randomized Clinical Trial," *Canadian Medical Association Journal*, Vol. 185, No. 9, 2013, pp. E409–E416.

Silberman, A., R. Banthia, I. S. Estay, C. Kemp, J. Studley, D. Hareras, and D. Ornish, "The Effectiveness and Efficacy of an Intensive Cardiac Rehabilitation Program in 24 Sites," *American Journal of Health Promotion*, Vol. 24, No. 4, 2010, pp. 260–266.

Silberstein, S. D., "Practice Parameter: Evidence-Based Guidelines for Migraine Headache (an Evidence-Based Review): Report of the Quality Standards Subcommittee of the American Academy of Neurology," *Neurology*, Vol. 55, No. 6, 2000, pp. 754–762.

South Carolina Code of Laws, Title 40, Chapter 31.

State of California, *Rules and Regulations*, "Board of Chiropractic Examiners, Editor," 2013a, p. 4.

———, *Business and Professions Code, Division 2, Chapter 8.2, Article 1*, "Naturopathic Doctors Act," Section 3613, 2013b.

———, *Business and Professions Code Section 4935–4949,* "Acupuncture Certification Requirements," Section 4937, 2014a.

———, *Business and Professions Code, Division 2, Chapter 10.5*, "Massage Therapy Act," Section 4611, 2014b.

State of Texas. *Occupations Code—Chapter 455 Massage Therapy,* Subchapter A. General Provisions. Section 455.001-3, 1999.

———, *Texas Occupations Code—Chapter 205 Acupuncture*, 2011a, p. 1.

———, *Occupations Code—Chapter 201 Chiropractors,* Subchapter A. General Provisions, Section 201.002, 2011b.

———. *Board Rules*, Texas Administrative Code, Title 22, Part 9, Chapter 183, Rule §183.7, 2014.

Stumpf, S., "Acupuncture Practice Acts: A Profession's Growing Pains," *Explore*, Vol. 11, No. 3, May–June 2015, pp. 217–221.

Texas Association of Naturopathic Doctors. *FAQ*, 2014.

Toward Optimized Practice. *Guideline for the Evidence-Informed Primary Care Management of Low Back Pain*, 2011.

TRICARE, *Tricare*, 2014a.

———, *Tricare Provider Handbook*, 2014b.

UK BEAM Trial Team, "United Kingdom Back Pain Exercise and Manipulation (UK BEAM) Randomised Trial: Effectiveness of Physical Treatments for Back Pain in Primary Care," *British Medical Journal*, Vol. 329, No. 7479, 2004, p. 1377–1384.

University of Texas. *Management of Fibromyalgia Syndrome in Adults*, Family Nurse Practitioner Program, 2009.

U.S. Department of Veterans Affairs, *Pre-Authorized Outpatient Medical Care*, 2011.

Vojta, D., J. De Sa, T. Prospect, and S. Stevens, "Effective Interventions for Stemming the Growing Crisis of Diabetes and Prediabetes: A National Payer's Perspective," *Health Affairs*, Vol. 31, No. 1, 2012, pp. 20–26.

Weeks, J., "Chiropractic Doctors Hit a Trifecta in Move for 'Cultural Authority'," *The Integrator Blog*, 2013.

Wickizer, T. M., G. Franklin, R. Plaeger-Brockway, and R. D. Mootz, "Improving the Quality of Workers' Compensation Health Care Delivery: The Washington State Occupational Health Services Project," *Milbank Quarterly*, Vol. 79, No. 1, 2001, pp. 5–33.

Wickizer, T. M., G. Franklin, J. V. Gluck, and D. Fulton-Kehoe, "Improving Quality Through Identifying Inappropriate Care: The Use of Guideline-Based Utilization Review Protocols in the Washington State Workers' Compensation System," *Journal of Occupational and Environmental Medicine*, Vol. 46, No. 3, 2004, pp. 198–204.